ESSENTIALS FOR PRINCIPALS

Mobile Learning Devices

KIPP D. ROGERS

A Joint Publication

D1468585

555 North Morton Street
Bloomington, IN 47404
800.733.6786 (toll free) / 812.336.7700
FAX: 812.336.7790

email: info@solution-tree.com
solution-tree.com

Visit **go.solution-tree.com/technology** to download the reproducibles in this book.

Printed in the United States of America

15 14 13 12 11   1 2 3 4 5

FSC
Mixed Sources
Product group from well-managed
forests and other controlled sources
Cert no. SW-COC-002283
www.fsc.org
© 1996 Forest Stewardship Council

Library of Congress Cataloging-in-Publication Data

Rogers, Kipp D.

Mobile learning devices / Kipp D. Rogers.

p. cm.

Includes bibliographical references.

ISBN 978-1-935542-69-8 (perfect bound) -- ISBN 978-1-935542-70-4 (library edition) 1. Mobile communication systems in education. 2. Educational technology. 3. Education--Effect of technological innovations on. I. Title.

LB1044.84.R64 2011

371.33--dc23

2011019666

Solution Tree
Jeffrey C. Jones, CEO & President

Solution Tree Press
President: Douglas M. Rife
Publisher: Robert D. Clouse
Vice President of Production: Gretchen Knapp
Managing Production Editor: Caroline Wise
Senior Production Editor: Edward M. Levy
Text Designer: Jenn Taylor
Cover Designer: Amy Shock

This book is dedicated to all of my little brothers who have great potential and who, for whatever reason, fail to realize it until someone looks them in the eye and says, "You can do it."

ACKNOWLEDGMENTS

I could easily fill every page of this book with the names and stories of people who have supported and encouraged me to complete it. I have been exceedingly and abundantly blessed, and for that I am so grateful. Yes, my help cometh from the Lord. I have to thank my mother, Portia, for being so proud of me and bragging every chance she gets, not to be outdone by my two aunts, Gloria and Arlene, who still believe that God has even more in store for me.

I especially want to thank my mother-in-law, Claretta Smith, for being my proofreader and for giving me constructive criticism and feedback. I am very grateful to my father-in-law, Crawford Smith, for his encouragement and gardening skills when I didn't have time to even cut my grass. Particular thanks go to Douglas Rife, president of Solution Tree Press, one of the people who looked me in the eye and said, "You can do it." I am also indebted to Dr. Steven Edwards, who has been a tremendous mentor for me. I also wish to thank Dr. Travis Twiford for encouraging me to continue to try to write and to publish educational literature. I have to give a big shout-out to my little brothers, Dr. Kianga Thomas and John Tupponce, for their support.

My Doodlebug, Rachel, and Big Man, Ryan, knew just when to come into the dining room to give me a hug or a kiss when I was working. It was just enough to keep me going. Finally, I thank my wife, Millicent, who is my strongest supporter and best friend. She has put up with many nights and weekends of my being attached to the computer, conducting research for this project, and did so without complaining. Thanks for repeatedly looking me in the eye and saying, "You can do it."

*   *   *

Solution Tree Press would like to thank the following reviewers:

Mark Abbondanza
Principal
North Strabane Intermediate School
Cannonsburg, Pennsylvania

William Ferriter
Sixth-Grade Language Arts Teacher
North Carolina

Mark Hofer
Associate Professor, School of Education
College of William and Mary
Williamsburg, Virginia

Elizabeth F. Keren-Kolb
Research Associate, Department of Teacher
    Education
University of Michigan
Ann Arbor, Michigan

Teresa Miller
Associate Professor, Department of
  Educational Leadership
Kansas State University
Manhattan, Kansas

Alice Owen
Executive Director of Technology
Irving Independent School District
Irving, Texas

Mike Ribble
District Director of Technology
Manhattan High School West/East Campus
Manhattan-Ogden School District
Manhattan, Kansas

Eric Sheninger
Principal
New Milford High School
New Milford, New Jersey

Greg Taranto
Principal
Cannonsburg Middle School
Cannonsburg, Pennsylvania

Tammy Worcester
Instructional Technology Specialist
Educational Services and Staff Development
  Council of Central Kansas
Hutchison, Kansas

TABLE OF CONTENTS

Reproducible pages are in italics.
Visit **go.solution-tree.com/technology** to download the reproducibles in this book.

ABOUT THE AUTHOR

Kipp Rogers, PhD, is director of secondary instruction for York County Schools in Virginia and owner of 21C3 Leadership Development. With nearly twenty years of experience in education, he has classroom teaching and instructional leadership experience at all levels in urban and suburban schools. Under his leadership, staff achieved high levels of professional learning and meaningful collaboration after looking at data, integrating technology, and differentiating instruction. Those significant efforts resulted in increased student performance in reading, writing, and math.

Kipp has presented at national conferences and has conducted workshops in several states. His presentations focus on strategies that integrate technology to promote student achievement and close achievement gaps. He received an international Leadership and Vision Award for his work using mobile learning devices (MLDs) as instructional tools, and he is the author of articles and books on mobile learning and integrating technology into instruction.

Kipp earned a bachelor's degree from Virginia State University, a master's from Old Dominion University, and a doctorate from Virginia Tech.

To book Kipp for professional development, contact pd@solution-tree.com

INTRODUCTION

Can you imagine going a day without your cell phone? If you left it at home while on your way to work, wouldn't you turn around to get it? Today's technological advances have made cell phones and mobile learning devices (MLDs) pervasive. As a result, it should come as no surprise that the use of MLDs—especially cell phones— in education has become a hotly debated topic. Some suggest that MLDs have no place in schools and are an extreme distraction. Others embrace and capitalize on their possibilities and use MLDs for instructional purposes. Both sides have legitimate points.

Advocates cite the advantages of the real-world tools these devices contain (such as calendars, calculators, note-taking functions, and cameras) and their ability to improve student attention and focus (Project Tomorrow, 2010). Conversely, others believe that cell phones and other MLDs add to and even exacerbate existing problems in schools—that they are not only a distraction, but that they perpetuate cheating and make it easier for students to cause trouble and participate in illegal activities. Many school administrators can't imagine students using cell phones for purposes other than texting their classmates the answers to tests, socializing, and taking inappropriate pictures and videos during school hours. Many educators are just not comfortable with technology. They fear that they will break something. Another factor is that, though they may want to find purpose and make connections within the existing curriculum, they do not want "something else to do."

Most educational leaders, however, realize that mobile learning is here to stay in education, so the question remains, How do we make it work? The purpose of this *Essential for Principals* guide is both to answer basic questions about implementing mobile learning in schools and to encourage educators to embrace mobile technology integration in the classroom. In the chapters that follow, we hope to provide a framework for understanding mobile learning and technology and research-based instructional strategies to use when leveraging mobile learning and technology to increase student motivation and achievement.

In chapter 1, we look at the nature of mobile learning, its benefits for schools, and the implications of the shift in our society from hard-wired computing (e-learning) to mobile learning (m-learning). In chapter 2, we investigate instructional pedagogy as it relates to mobile learning. In particular, we will look at national standards, skills, and research-based instructional strategies that should be used when integrating mobile learning in schools. In chapter 3, we offer a model for technology integration and share strategies and ideas for managing classrooms when using MLDs. Chapter 4 offers specific steps for getting started with mobile learning in schools and includes guidance for home communication, acceptable-use policies, and surveys.

Ideas and lesson plans for integrating MLDs into the classroom are the subject of chapter 5. There you will find complete lesson plans for nine different types of MLDs. Reproducible versions of these lesson plans can also be downloaded at **go.solution-tree com/technology** or photocopied from the appendix. Finally, in chapter 6, we look at the implications of mobile learning devices for instruction and the potential they have to assist with educational reform.

CHAPTER 1

Learning Every Time, Everywhere

I will never forget the day that one of my teachers flew into my office, exclaiming, "Mr. Rogers, I took this cell phone from Chante.' She had it on in class, and she was text messaging. I caught her red-handed, so I took the phone! Do you want it?"

Four years ago, my reaction to this situation would have been to take the phone and keep it until a parent came to school. Cell phones were becoming a nuisance for teachers and my assistant principals. What changed my mind? Reality. Digital natives, 21st century learners, generation D, or generation text—whatever you choose to call them, this generation of students is ready to learn differently, and future generations are right behind them. While Chante's behavior was inappropriate, the truth of the matter is that she was just passing notes in class, 21st-century style (Rogers, 2009a).

As a middle school principal of almost eleven hundred sixth-, seventh- and eighth-grade students, and the father of a cell phone–toting eighth grader, it did not take long for me to realize that most middle school students had cell phones. If they did not, they would the next time there was a holiday or gift-giving occasion in their lives. A study by CTIA: The Wireless Association and Harris Interactive (2008) indicated that seventeen million, or four out of five teenagers, were carrying cell phones in 2008 and that this number was steadily rising. If 80 percent of our students now own cell phones, we as educators are fighting a losing battle to keep phones and other mobile learning devices out of school. We should be turning these perceived obstacles into opportunities to learn.

I was not always convinced of this. In my early years as a middle school principal, I was all over kids who wore ear buds or played with handheld games during the instructional day. I just did not get why kids needed to use these tools during school. The administrative instinct is to take them away, to be returned only if a parent comes to the school to claim the confiscated item. I remained a nonbeliever until I had the opportunity to help teach a seventh-grade pre-algebra class. This was the most rewarding—and humbling—experience that I have ever had as an administrator, especially since my subject of expertise is science. Talk about a learning curve!

The class held an interesting mix of personalities and academic abilities. Like other schools, ours typically adjusted instruction to accommodate student needs based on a quarterly assessment.

Our leadership team decided to give all students the math assessment on the same day. The assessment required the use of a calculator, and in a school that housed nearly eleven hundred students, that presented a logistical challenge to say the least. We didn't have enough calculators for all of the students to take the test at the same time.

Although I borrowed several calculators from my peers, we were still short a few, so I let one of the students use the calculator on my smartphone. The student remarked to me that he had a calculator on his own phone that he wasn't allowed to use. The other students chimed in. I took advantage of the teachable moment and discovered that nineteen of twenty-two students in the class either owned or had access to cell phones—and therefore to electronic calculators. That got us started using cell phones in the classroom, and it sparked my interest in mobile learning.

Mobile learning technology is now a part of our culture, and educators must learn how to use it to help students achieve.

What Is Mobile Learning, and Why Use It?

Mobile technology is found everywhere you look, in the form of cell phones, personal digital assistants (PDAs), MP3 players (so-called because they were developed by Moving Pictures Experts Group), handheld games, digital audio players, and laptops. We are all intrigued by the ability to carry photos, music, documents, and even books on the phones in our pockets or clipped to our belts. Mobile learning is the delivery of learning anytime, anywhere, using these amazing technologies (Goh & Hooper, 2007; Wagner & Robson, 2005). Today's "digital natives," as Marc Prensky (2005) dubbed them, are accustomed to instant access, immediate feedback, and the ability to obtain information at will.

Rashid Aderinoye, K. O. Ojokheta, and A. A. Olojede (2007) have referred to m-learning as a novel educational approach that encourages flexibility. Students do not have to fit a specific mold to participate. Restrictions of time, space, and place are lifted. Mobile learning is portable, discrete, and adaptable to the learners' evolving skills and knowledge—all characteristics that drive students' curiosity. Ray Schroeder predicted in 2005 that by 2008, mobile learning would expand and evolve dramatically and that e-learners would no longer be chained to their computers (Schroeder, 2005). They would learn, he predicted, while hiking in the mountains, jogging, or strolling along a beach. I would venture to say that Schroeder's prediction was accurate. If you take time to observe students outside of an educational setting, you are bound to see many of them interacting with some sort of mobile devices in unusual places. For example, I recently took my children to the Smithsonian National Zoo. I observed four students at different exhibits taking photos with iPod touches (iPods with high-resolution displays) of some of the animals and facts that were displayed. I asked one young lady what she was going to do with the pictures. She indicated that she was going to use them to write a report on her visit and that she was going to start writing the report on the bus ride home.

Thus, mobile learning allows teaching and learning to extend beyond the walls of a traditional classroom (Kaser, 2009; Kolb, 2006; McGuire, 2005; New Media Consortium & EDUCAUSE

Learning Initiative, 2007). It allows teachers as well as students to break the tether of the desktop computer. In fact, the term *classroom* itself is becoming antiquated. Perhaps *collabroom* would be more appropriate.

m-learning devices are novel, powerful, and fun; they perform functions that make our lives easier; they complete tasks in a fraction of the time they would otherwise take. A less obvious reason to incorporate mobile learning in everyday instruction is its instructional and pedagogical value. The next chapter will focus on the sound instructional pedagogy that MLDs can support.

From e-Learning to m-Learning

I recently attended a family friend's surprise fortieth birthday party and talked to one of the guests, a soldier, about his tour in Korea. He told me that Koreans used cell phones to complete banking transactions and pay for food and public transportation. He noted that several third-world countries have skipped right over using computers and gone mobile directly.

It's true that some countries that are using mobile technologies as a way of life do not have the infrastructure to support desktop computers (e-learning) and hard-wired technology. Although e-learning still has a strong presence, especially in North America, the shift to methods that are essentially free from boundaries is occurring quickly. The world is moving toward a totally wireless economy—what I've heard referred to as a "mobiconomy."

Ali Mostakhdemin-Hosseini and Jarno Tuimala (2005) identify mobile learning as the natural evolution of e-learning—that is, any learning that takes place in an electronic environment. In many cases, e-learning is supported by m-learning—for example, when learners do not have quick access to nonmovable technical devices (Charmonman & Chorpothong, 2005). It has also been suggested (Wang, Wu, & Wang, 2009) that the rapidly growing electronic learning market will be enhanced by the proliferation of mobile computing, since m-learners are able to utilize electronic resources while away from traditional learning places.

On the flip side, some researchers contend that there are too many barriers for mobile devices to replace traditional learning (Motiwalla, 2007; Wang et al., 2009). These barriers include small screens, limited connectivity and input capabilities, short battery life, data storage and transaction errors, less surf ability, and graphics limitations. For these reasons, the researchers contend, m-learning may be slower to catch on and may limit learning opportunities, especially in areas where e-learning is already widespread.

However, the interest in mobile technology, and more specifically mobile phones, is growing daily among all segments of the population. In fact, the number of children ages four to fourteen who own mobile devices has grown by double digits since 2005 (Shuler, 2009). My seven-year-old daughter Rachel knows how to use my phone (when I'm not looking) to take pictures of herself, her brother, and her lunch, as well as to play games. She can use the calculator to check her homework. My mother, who is seventy-seven, knows how to send a text message—a skill that I selfishly taught her because I always felt a wave of anxiety when she called me during the workday.

Because mobile learning devices appeal across age groups, they break communication barriers and create lifelong learning opportunities (Wagner & Robson, 2005). m-Learning also changes student-to-student and student-to-teacher relationships: It allows students to collaborate more easily and frequently and can enhance student and teacher interaction, especially for students who do not readily raise their hands in class to ask a question for fear of feeling stupid. Using communication tools that students like minimizes the digital divide between teachers and students (Brown, 2003). Think about it. When students use mobile technology, they are at the center of their learning and in charge of the content.

Bryan Alexander (2004) implies that m-learning represents a shift from anywhere, anytime to everywhere, every time. Computers are increasingly becoming smaller, lighter, and more powerful and affordable for individuals and school districts. As a result of the portability of mobile learning devices like laptops, school districts have invested in classroom sets—often referred to as COWs (computers on wheels)—freeing up much-needed classroom space. And school districts are now investing in one-to-one laptop computer initiatives to further opportunities for students to learn outside of the four walls of school. Having COWs and one-to-one computer initiatives allows students to use technology in a setting that is not a computer lab, and so, theoretically, is a form of m-learning. Netbooks, which are lightweight, sturdy, and inexpensive to replace if broken, have served as a good alternative for several school districts.

Another advantage of m-learning over e-learning is that the long-term cost of infrastructure for hard-wired e-learning can be expensive. Moreover, computers are almost outdated by the time students get them, not to mention after the typical three-year recycling schedule. Shifting to a more mobile and less costly platform of e-learning can mediate the expense of building digital literacy.

The Ubiquity of m-Learning

In 2009, Carly Shuler reported that 93 percent of children in the United States had access to a mobile device. She also indicated that more than half of children ages six-to-nine-years old had a mobile device of their own. Schools districts have begun to recognize this growing trend. They are making an effort to understand the benefits and potential impact of mobile learning on instruction and have started to purchase mobile learning devices for use in classrooms.

In education, the ubiquity of mobile learning devices encourages flexibility and freedom. It also commands a different way of thinking about how to plan for and deliver educational content. The prevalence of mobile technology may in fact drive the manner in which kids want to be taught. No wonder researchers like Dale Spender (2007) have reported a divide between traditional teaching strategies and contemporary youth attitudes. Joseph Rene Corbeil and Maria Elena Valdes-Corbeil (2007) attempt to narrow this divide by arguing that by using m-learning, teachers can interact with and access students while on the go. Kristine Peters (2007) suggests that m-learning creates learning opportunities that are different than those acquired via e-learning (desktop computers). Other researchers like Laura Naismith, Peter Lonsdale, Giasemi Vavoula, and Mike Sharples (2004) also help educators leverage the ubiquity of m-learning by suggesting it has an impact on learning by centering on the individual learner's environment as opposed to the classroom, by involving learners in making connections to various resources and other people, and by allowing learners to instantly publish their observations and creations.

Because of its ubiquity, mobile information is quickly becoming an important enabler of the new social structure. In other words, as a result of new technology and innovation, geographical proximity no longer identifies communities (Peters, 2007). The speed with which we are able to access communication and information via portable technology helps to form social structures that are based upon personal interest and jobs. As Julia Fallon (2008) states, because of the ubiquity of m-learning and mobile learning devices, students of today do not experience geographical place and time as barriers to learning.

Technological and Social Change

When my son was in sixth grade, I walked into our family room one afternoon and, without his knowing, observed him for a few minutes. He was watching television, interacting on a social network (www.gaiaonline.com), talking to one friend on his cell phone, texting another, and listening to music on the computer. I said, "Ryan, you need to turn something off or stop doing something— you can't possibly be paying attention to all of this." He immediately replied by telling me what SpongeBob was doing, whom he was communicating with on Gaia, what he and his friend were discussing on the phone (Gaia stuff), what he was texting, and the name and artist of the song that was playing. Needless to say, he is a typical digital native and is aware of what is going on with all of the digital stimulation he has initiated.

On another occasion, I was on an airplane flying to San Diego to conduct a cell phone workshop at a national conference. I sat next to a gentleman on a two-hour leg of the journey. It was early, and neither of us spoke other than to say a cordial good morning. After the plane landed, I noticed that he was singing softly to himself. So I asked, "Are you in a band?"

"Kind of," the man replied. "I'm not sure if you watch *American Idol,* but I was a contestant. I was voted off, but I got a wild card, so I'm flying back to Los Angeles to tape the show."

I was impressed. I was sitting next to someone who was potentially the next *American Idol* pop star. As I walked through the airport, I pulled out my smartphone and did a quick Google search of the young man. Sure enough, his name came up as a contestant. I then went to YouTube to see if I could hear him. Sure enough, someone had posted one of his performances. He had a great voice. Anytime, anywhere learning—or better yet, everywhere, everytime learning. The reality is that because of mobile devices, students can do the same thing that I did. They can use mobile devices to investigate questions they raise and take charge of their own learning. If students are curious about a topic and want to learn something new, they can do so at a moment's notice.

The mobile revolution is not coming; it's already here. Evidence of mobile penetration is everywhere. Not having a cell phone is now almost unheard of in the United States, regardless of age; this is quickly becoming true for other forms of MLDs as well. A study conducted in 2007 by Felix Librero, Juan Angelo Ramos, Adelina I. Ranga, Jerome Triñona, and David Lambert indicated that one and a half billion people had powerful computers in their pockets and purses—in the form of cell phones. Moreover, today's top-of-the-line cell phones, more often referred to as smartphones (iPhone, Palm, and BlackBerry, for example), have the computing power of personal computers from the 1990s. And our culture is such that whenever a new piece of mobile technology comes out, we run right out to get it. Look at the iPad. People waited in line for hours to get one. The end result? Over three million were sold in the first eighty days of its release.

According to Alan Moore and Tomi Ahonen (2004), there are nearly four billion mobile phone subscriptions in the world, meaning that three billion people carry 1.4 mobile phones wherever they go. Three billion people send short message service (SMS) text messages daily. Nielson Mobile (2007) indicated that in 2007, 57 percent of mobile subscribers in the United States texted daily. (Other countries reached this statistic in 2003.) The United States sent over one trillion text messages in 2008, and that number continues to grow.

In several countries in the world, the cell phone is in fact the main form of communication. Not only Korea, but the United Kingdom, the Netherlands, Finland, Taiwan, and many countries in Africa use cell phones in commerce and learning quite frequently. They are used to teach English, history, and science. In Japan, cell phones have limited but standard Internet access and email; according to an April 2000 study, only 17 percent of participants in Japan had home access to a computer, while 100 percent owned mobile phones (Thornton & Houser, 2005).

The "iPhamily Phenomenon," or infiltration of Apple's iPods, iPod touch, and iPads, nearly single-handedly changed the mobile learning culture. In September of 2009, nearly 40 percent of 58 million iPhone devices sold were iPod touches. Today 29.3 million people in the U.S. own a Nintendo DS, a handheld game system that can also be used as a mobile learning device.

Digital Equity

Generation text is accustomed to learning via multimedia. Television, handheld games, Internet, and yes, cell phones all work in concert to help shape their learning and their literacy. The 21st century learner tends to use pictures and sound to learn (Wagner & Robinson, 2005). These learners are digitally literate, mobile, always on, and experiential.

In 2006, nearly 100 percent of students ages twelve to seventeen either owned or had access to some type of mobile learning device (McNeal & van't Hooft, 2006). In 2008, over 80 percent of students in the United States ages twelve to seventeen owned cell phones (Common Sense Media, 2010; CTIA: The Wireless Association & Harris Interactive, 2008; Deubel, 2009; Kolb, 2008; Rideout, Foehr, & Roberts, 2010; Soloway, Norris, & Cooper, 2009). However, this statistic also means that roughly 20 percent do not own these tools.

What can educators do to compensate for the inequity? Group activities can be created to incorporate shared MLDs. It's best that these groups be kept small; two or three students to a device is probably best; however, I have found that students work well with only one cell phone in groups of three or four. In fact, I recommend that the first few times cell phones or other mobile devices are used in classrooms, the activities should be conducted using collaborative groups. This way, the teacher can become accustomed to the management of the tools. Having students work initially in cooperative learning groups will also help to eliminate peer pressure for those students who do not have their own device. "If only the teacher has a cell phone," Liz Kolb (2008, p. 14) writes, "the students can use that one cell phone to do the activities." Using a single cell phone is particularly useful in elementary schools, where the number of students who own them is naturally lower than it is in secondary schools.

Even when students may not have Internet access at home and therefore cannot conduct research to complete assignments, most have access to a cell phone, iPod touch, or MP3 player via a family member at home, and they can be taught to use what they have to complete research and homework assignments. I have found that most students who own cell phones utilize text messaging more often than they talk on the phone. This is in keeping with a study conducted in 2009 by PEW Internet (Lenhart, Ling, Campbell, & Purcell, 2010) which found that 54 percent of teens contact their friends via text message daily as opposed to only 38 percent of teens who call their friends on cell phones. Even less (30 percent) call friends on landlines. Text messaging is quick, discreet, and inexpensive. Of the 200 or so students who piloted the use of cell phones in our school, 176 (88 percent) owned their own cell phone and 170 (80 percent) had unlimited text messaging as part of their monthly plans. Not surprisingly, 100 percent of students either owned or had access to a cell phone, MP3 player, or handheld game. However, access for students who have their own mobile learning devices can sometimes be affected by matters beyond teacher control. When students have their cell phones confiscated by parents as a form of discipline, that can hinder participation in cell phone activities in and outside of class. In fact, this was usually the only reason students failed to bring their cell phone to my class. I don't recall ever hearing a student say, "I left my cell phone at home."

An option for teachers who have classes in which there are too few cell phones available is to ask family members or coworkers to donate their old cell phones. Another option is to ask a local cell phone company to donate a few older phones for class activities. In these cases, the cell phones will not be able to access SMS text messaging; however, students will still be able to use several of the peripherals, such as the camera, video camera, notepad, calculator, calendar, and voice recorder. And if the cell phone has Bluetooth, many items can be beamed to other students in class who have text messaging and multimedia messaging service (MMS) capabilities. Multimedia messaging allows the user to send and receive photos, video, and audio via text message.

Nearly two years after experimenting with my group of seventh graders, I had convinced several other teachers to begin using cell phones, iPods, iPod touches, MP3 players, and even Nintendo DSs as instructional tools. I don't think I will ever forget the energy and excitement that students exhibited in a sixth-grade classroom I visited that was in the middle of a language arts activity involving cell phones. The students were using their phones to text phrases to polleverywhere.com to create a humorous poem using onomatopoeia. They were working in groups of two and three, all on task and all engaged. One student said it was fun—and that he was also paying more attention.

Benefits and Challenges

Let's take a closer look at the benefits and challenges of using mobile learning devices for instruction.

Benefits

I have identified eight core pedagogical benefits of using mobile learning devices with instruction:

1. **Improved pedagogy**—When teachers use technology as part of instruction, they increase the likelihood that their teaching skills will be effective and that student achievement will improve.

2. **Deeper student motivation**—Because MLDs are fun, they encourage student motivation and participation. Students use their mobile learning devices to play games independently and with friends. They use laptops to communicate with friends via social networking sites like Facebook and MySpace. Students publish self-created art forms, including poetry, music, and skits to social networking sites like YouTube. The feedback they get from their peers assists them in improving their skills and enhances their motivation to improve. This feedback increases what Retta Guy (2009) refers to as "social capital" and can in turn motivate all students, especially those who are deemed to be at risk.

3. **Access to content and decreasing the access gap**—Since many low-income families can't afford the monthly cost of Internet service, many students have cell phones, iPods, MP3 players, or handheld gaming devices that allow access to outside research via text messaging or Wi-Fi. MLDs provide extremely convenient access to material inside and outside the four walls of schools. For example, students can use MLDs while on field trips to extend learning, ask questions, and clarify information. The potential for narrowing the access gap is tremendous, lines of equity are blurred, and students can solve problems in the environment where they happen to be. For example, students can use their cell phones or iPod touches to video short public service announcements to discourage bullying or to encourage recycling. The videos can be shared on student announcements.

4. **Easy review of content**—MLDs provide a convenient way to review material for busy students and teachers and can be used to contain training modules to teach a specific skill. McDonald's uses iPod touches to train its staff (Spriggs, 2010). Think about it! A student on a long bus ride to or from school can review vocabulary words while listening to his favorite music.

5. **Augmented student-driven learning**—With MLDs, students have convenient access to content and material that interests them, when it interests them. One of the highest forms of learning takes place when students have a vested interest in or buy-in to the content they are learning (Jensen, 2008). For example, if a student who plays piano is learning about a musician, he might use his device to find something on YouTube about that musician, as I did with my seatmate on the plane ride, or even to learn how to play one of the musician's songs.

6. **Personalized, differentiated learning**—In many cases, students are able to use MLDs to personalize their own learning and choose the manner (or media) that suits their learning style. If a student is an auditory learner, she can listen to a podcast. If she is a visual learner, she can watch a video. If he is a spatial learner, he can play a game.

7. **Increased collaborative learning**—Most classrooms don't have a complete set of any technological device. That is typically the case with MLDs. As a result, students are forced to communicate with each other to plan and produce a product.

8. **Improved communication**—Relationships between teacher and student improve as a result of the teacher embracing the student's culture. Communication barriers are broken. Teachers learn to talk the talk and text the text (Brown, 2003; Çavus, Bicen, & Akçil, 2008; Deubel, 2009; Rismark, Sølverg, Strømme, & Hokstad, 2007).

Challenges

I have identified ten challenges to using MLDs as part of instruction.

1. **Affordability**—Although MLDs are nearly ubiquitous, not all students can afford them. Educators need to take this problem into consideration. MLDs can also be relatively expensive. Cell phones usually come with a monthly plan, and iPods are a couple of hundred dollars. Many of the applications come with a cost as well.

2. **Device size and screen "real estate"**—Portability has a price. Typically, mobile device screens are considerably smaller than regular computer screens. This difference is one of the important challenges for educators (Dodds & Mason 2005; Duke Center for Instructional Technology, 2008; McNeal & van 't Hooft, 2006; Prensky, 2005; Shuler, 2009). The limited screen size requires more scrolling, which many users find cumbersome (Presnky, 2005). To compensate for small screen real estate, these tools rely on rich media that combine text, graphics, audio, and video. The effectiveness of these compensations, in turn, is affected by issues such as connectivity, which is dictated by the technology available, such as Bluetooth and Wi-Fi. Watching a YouTube video may be subject to download times and connectivity speeds; viewing may be choppy, with poor sound quality.

   In many cases, MLD screens are too small for more than two students to share at one time. However, more elaborate tools have considerably larger screens. This is one of the reasons that my personal favorite is a netbook or iPad. Both have portability but larger screens.

3. **Device security**—Because the devices are small, they have a tendency to "grow legs" and "walk," unless specific procedures are put in place for their use in school settings. If students are using their own devices, it is not as much of an issue, but if students are using school hardware like iPods or MP3 players, a rigorous system of distribution and retrieval is needed. Each MLD should be clearly marked with the school's name and assigned a number.

4. **Variability of devices**—When students use their own cell phones, it's often like having a melting pot of technology in the class. One of my science teachers who used cell phones quite frequently in class had several students with different service providers. If they were doing an activity that required them to text, they would have to huddle in groups of people who had the same service. You would see the AT&T kids in one corner, the Verizon kids in another corner, and the T-Mobile kids somewhere else in his windowless classroom.

Different cell phones also have different peripherals, such as voice recorders, video cameras, and calculators. Teachers definitely need to consider these issues when designing lessons.

5. **Digital citizenship (appropriate use)**—Using MLDs appropriately is probably one of the more pressing concerns of educators today (Johnson & Kritsonis, 2007; Mario, 2008; Rogers, 2009b; Shuler, 2009; Teaching Today, n.d.). In general, students just don't have a good concept of what they should and should not be doing with mobile devices. For instance, some students at my school videotaped a fight between two students at a bus stop, and someone posted the video on YouTube. The interesting thing about the incident was that the young lady who posted the video did not see anything wrong with it. The challenge is getting students to understand that while the jury is out on the legality of posting videos of people (especially ones that are humiliating) without their permission, it is nevertheless morally wrong. For example, look at www.Walmart-people.com. This site posts pictures of unsuspecting shoppers in less than flattering outfits and hairstyles. Whenever possible, educators should talk to students about appropriate use and etiquette. Once a video is posted on the Internet, it is technically available forever. We also have to model as well as teach appropriate use. I am always surprised when I see adults answering phones during meetings—and sometimes even holding conversations. Assume nothing, and teach everything. I have to remind my son and daughter sometimes when we are out at dinner not to answer a text message or play a video game.

6. **Cyberbullying**—In California, a woman was accused of helping her daughter create a fictitious MySpace account with the purpose of harassing a neighbor (Neil, 2008). The incident ended in the neighbor committing suicide. Let's face it, technology does make it easier for the bully. The good news is that digital footprints also make it easier for the cyberbully to be caught. In 1984, the state of Virginia enacted the Computer Crimes Act, which prohibits causing physical injury to another through the use of a computer or computer network. Unfortunately, cyberbullying is similar to regular bullying in that students and educators are often unaware when they are being subjected to cyberbullying or even what it is (Strom & Strom, 2005). My recommendation is to find a good acceptable-use policy that specifically addresses cyberbullying.

7. **"Sexting"**—Many students don't think anything is wrong with texting sexually suggestive messages and pictures to each other. They don't consider the "what ifs." But what happens when in five years the inappropriate photo ends up posted on several websites? In Ohio, a high school student committed suicide after she was teased about a nude photo that she sent to her boyfriend (Celizic, 2009). It is extremely important to review digital safety and to have frank discussions about digital footprints.

8. **Cheating**—Some students cheat with pencils and paper, and those students will cheat with MLDs, too. Many can text without looking at the keyboard of the phone, just as most of us can with a regular computer keyboard. Many can send a text message with the device still in their pockets! Teachers also fear that students will take pictures of answer keys or test contents and send them to friends (Stansbury, 2008). When a teacher tells me that students can text answers to tests to students in other classes, my response is that students can just

as easily share an answer to a test during lunch without the use of technology. We need to look at a different form of assessment that makes cheating more difficult. For example, instead of giving a multiple-choice test, give a problem-based assessment, or ask students to create a product that demonstrates mastery of the skill that was taught. Other ways to control the problem of cheating using cell phones is to have students put their cell phones on top of their desks during the test or to collect the cell phones prior to the test and then return them after the test is completed.

9. **Distraction**—Technology can distract students when instruction is being delivered by traditional methods. For example, some will listen to music during a lecture or play a video game instead of working on an assignment. But we must also ask, for whom is this behavior distracting? Kids have an uncanny ability to multitask. Granted, some studies argue that the knowledge attained is not as deep when students are focused on too many things at once (Richtel, 2004; Stansbury, 2008). I do think there should be limits to multitasking, especially for younger students. However, there should also be exceptions. For instance, many students indicate that they are able to focus better if they have music playing as they work. I happen to be one of them.

10. **The digital divide**—Students who are more technologically advanced as a result of having more access may have an unfair advantage over those who are not as tech savvy. This advantage may transfer into differences in student achievement. A related challenge is that technology changes so rapidly that by the time a student masters a skill or program, it may be outdated.

Table 1.1 reiterates the benefits alongside some of the risks of mobile learning. Ultimately, when looking at them side by side, you have to ask yourself, do the benefits outweigh the risks? As a former principal who has used all types of MLDs in the classroom setting, I would say the risks are more of a problem for educators than they are for students. The key to minimizing the challenges of implementing MLDs in the school setting is to be upfront and honest with students about expectations of what is and is not appropriate use in the classroom. Isn't this true for anything? Mobile learning should not be any different.

Table 1.1: Instructional Benefits and Challenges of Mobile Learning

Challenges	Benefits
Affordability	Improves instructional pedagogy
Device size and screen real estate	Increases student motivation
Device security	Expands access to content
Variability of devices	Enables review content at will
Digital citizenship (appropriate use)	Augments student-driven learning
Cyberbullying	Personalizes differentiated learning
Sexting	Decreases the access gap
Cheating	Promotes collaborative learning
Distraction	Improves communication
Digital divide	

Enhancing the Curriculum

Technology does not replace good, solid instruction. Technology should never be the lead actor in the play; it should always be the supporting actor. I noticed as a principal that some educators use technology for its own sake and miss the bigger picture. However, many school districts are finding appropriate ways to integrate technology into the curriculum. For example, online curricula are often embedded with links to interesting websites that students can use to enhance what they are learning. MLDs can provide students and teachers just-in-time access to that information without disrupting the learning of other students. The mobile technology used should be suited to the particular learning task (see chapter 5).

In the next chapter, we take a closer look at the instructional and pedagogical purposes of using mobile learning devices in the classroom.

CHAPTER 2

Mobile Learning Technology and Instruction

With the increased availability of sophisticated mobile technology, such as high-powered smartphones, computer tablets, and handheld games, the value of mobile learning devices in school is being questioned less and less. Many educators would also agree that ubiquity itself is a good reason to use MLDs (Andone, Dron, Pemberton, & Boyne, 2007; Corbeil & Valdes-Corbeil, 2007; Deubel, 2009; Duke Center for Instructional Technology, 2008; Gilroy, 2004; Kolb, 2008; Sadik, 2008). However, this is not always enough to convince more conservative skeptics to bring these devices into the classroom. This chapter focuses on what may be more convincing—the instructional and pedagogical purposes of using MLDs in the classroom.

Teaching 21st Century Skills

Voices inside and outside the educational community are calling for more meaningful emphasis on 21st century learning outcomes, outcomes designed to focus on the skills that students need to be successful in work and in life.

What are 21st century skills? What are the national standards for teaching 21st century skills and mobile learning? Although definitions vary, most lists of 21st century skills require students to learn how to think creatively and how to make the best use of rapidly changing technologies. These critical-thinking skills are often referred to as "soft skills," skills that computers can't provide and that are considered crucial to working in a rapidly changing global society. Teaching 21st century skills doesn't necessarily mean using a lot of technology; sometimes it's simply a matter of approaching an assignment differently and allowing students to practice skills like teamwork, collaboration, and self-directed learning (Roberts & Foehr, 2008). Occasional implementation of technology—especially mobile technology—can be leveraged to facilitate 21st century skills such as communication, collaboration, and self-directed learning.

In practice, the term *21st century skills* has become a catch phrase that some educational organizations use to support any kind of teaching and learning. To counteract this vagueness, the Partnership for 21st Century Skills (2008) spent the better part of ten years identifying and standardizing the most comprehensive framework of skills students will need in order to be successful in work and in life in the 21st century (Kay, 2010). The Partnership's framework, which is focused on student outcomes, encompasses four essential areas:

1. Core subjects and 21st century themes

2. Life and career skills

3. Learning and innovation skills

4. Information, media, and technology skills

Ken Kay (2010), former president for the Partnership for 21st Century Skills, says that when students are exposed to 21st century skills in school and assessed on them regularly, they will be prepared to think, work, learn, solve problems, and contribute effectively throughout their lives.

When considering the 21st century skills that mobile learning devices can enhance, the area of learning and innovation seems to fit best. These are increasingly being recognized as the skills students will need to prepare for the workforce. Within the learning and innovation skill set of the Partnership's framework, there are some must-haves that should be deliberately incorporated within curricula and regularly assessed in the classroom. The Partnership refers to them as the four Cs: creativity, critical thinking, communication, and collaboration. (A detailed explanation of the four Cs can be found at www.21stcenturyskills.org.)

The four Cs are certainly not new or unique to the 21st century; however, consciously integrating them into the curriculum is. Table 2.1 shows the role that mobile learning devices can play in enhancing these skills.

Incorporating National Technology Standards

There is no hard and fast rule on what teaching 21st century skills looks like; however, national standards provide a good framework from which educators can work when designing lessons that utilize technology. Jay McTighe and Elliot Seif (2010) suggest implementing a framework of five components that results in students obtaining 21st century skills despite teachers' having to "teach the standards." The five interrelated components are (1) mission of schools, (2) principles of learning, (3) systems of curriculum and assessment, (4) instructional programs and practices, and (5) systemic support factors. McTighe and Seif suggest beginning by focusing on the school's mission and having that mission include language that speaks to 21st century outcomes. For example, when I was a middle school principal, our mission statement simply said, "Preparing 21st century learners for success in a global society." In ten words, we were able to convey a message that 21st century skills were important to our school. In working toward 21st century outcomes that are based on standards, the most widely accepted technology standards are the National Educational Technology Standards (NETS).

Table 2.1: How the Four Cs Are Supported by Mobile Learning

21st Century Skills	Skills That Mobile Learning Supports
Creativity and Innovation	• Brainstorm to use idea-creation techniques. • Elaborate, refine, analyze, and evaluate ideas to improve and maximize creative efforts.
Critical Thinking	• Reason effectively. • Analyze how parts of a whole interact with each other. • Make judgments and decisions. • Analyze and evaluate evidence, arguments, claims, and beliefs. • Analyze and evaluate major alternative points of view. • Synthesize and make connections between information and arguments. • Interpret information and draw conclusions. • Reflect critically on learning experiences and processes. • Solve problems. • Solve different kinds of nonfamiliar problems in both conventional and innovative ways. • Identify and ask significant questions that clarify various points of view and lead to better solutions.
Communication	• Articulate thoughts and ideas effectively using oral, written, and nonverbal communication skills. • Listen effectively to decipher meaning. • Use communication to inform, instruct, motivate, and persuade. • Utilize multiple media and technologies. • Communicate effectively in diverse environments.
Collaboration	• Demonstrate ability to work effectively and respectfully with diverse teams. • Exercise flexibility and willingness to be helpful in making necessary compromises to accomplish a common goal. • Assume shared responsibility for collaborative work, and value individual contributions made by team members.

The initial NETS, created in 1998, focused on students embracing and mastering technological tools; now that digital students are much more adept at using technology, however, the NETS focus on technological proficiency that comes as a result of e-learning and m-learning (International Society for Technology in Education, 2010)—that is, the focus of the current NETS for students is on digital fluency. The standards emphasize that students need to focus on authentic, inventive, and emergent uses of digital technology and on how they apply outside the school setting. The focus is more practice oriented than knowledge based and encourages educators to move from teaching students how to use the technology to teaching them how to use the technology to learn. This change in focus aligns with the orientation of the Partnership for 21st Century Skills.

These standards for students are being increasingly adopted around the world. The six skills that NETS emphasizes are the following:

1. Creativity and innovation

2. Communication and collaboration

3. Research and information fluency

4. Critical thinking, problem solving, and decision making

5. Digital citizenship

6. Technology operations and concepts

These six standards, as you can see, are not very different from the learning and innovation skills that are outlined in the Framework for 21st Century Skills (Kay, 2010). In fact, NETS simply extends the four Cs by adding research and informational literacy, digital citizenship (which is of great concern to educators as it relates to mobile learning), and technology operations and concepts. Let's look at these six standards one by one.

Creativity and Innovation

The creativity and innovation standard challenges educators to stimulate student creativity and innovation while meeting local and state content standards and objectives. One of the key 21st century skills for success in today's global market is the ability to work as a group and collaborate on projects with others.

With regard to this standard, students can do the following with mobile learning devices:

• Create a podcasted public service announcement about classroom or school rules that can be listened to on an MP3 player.

• Use the audio or video recording function to record a poem, short story, or original musical piece.

Communication and Collaboration

The second NETS for students standard is communication and collaboration. This standard emphasizes student use of digital media environments to communicate and work collaboratively, including at a distance, to support individual learning and to contribute to the learning of others. Students can:

• Use an iPad to access Google Docs to copublish a document with all members of a group.

• Use an MLD to access Twitter to communicate ideas with students in other countries.

• Use an MLD to upload pictures or text to a group blog.

An example of this standard in action would be to ask a class to collaborate on a project with a class in another school in another state or country. Blogs and wikis could be the medium that the class uses to contribute to the learning.

Research and Information Fluency

This standard emphasizes ways that students can apply digital tools to gather, evaluate, and use information. With MLDs, students can use the Google SMS function with their cell phones to gather basic information about a specific topic they are researching. With devices that have Internet access, students can use digital tools such as Google, Wikipedia, and YouTube to produce products and reports.

Critical Thinking, Problem Solving, and Decision Making

With mobile learning, students are able to use critical-thinking skills to plan and conduct research, manage projects, solve problems, and make informed decisions using appropriate digital tools and resources. For example, teachers can encourage critical thinking by showing a picture of the aftermath of the 2011 earthquake in Japan and by having students use their MLD to research and blog a response to the picture as it relates to what they are currently studying. Students can also use the camera and video functions on their devices to capture and analyze data to make informed decisions and solve problems. For example, students can use the video function on their MLD to create a public service announcement that encourages students to recycle lunch trash. Students can also use the calendar function on some mobile learning devices (such as cell phones or iPod touches) to plan and manage activities and to make decisions based on timelines.

Digital Citizenship

This standard emphasizes the human, cultural, and societal issues related to technology and the practice of legal and ethical behavior by focusing on digital safety prior to using the mobile learning device. Students can also assist with developing policies for acceptable and appropriate MLD use in the school and classroom.

Technology Operations and Concepts

This standard emphasizes development of a sound understanding of technology concepts, systems, and operations (Setzer, 2008; Stockwell, 2007). For example, students can apply their current knowledge of computer use to take a photograph using their cell phones and to upload it to a website, download it to their desktop computer, and then import it into a PowerPoint presentation. The information given in table 2.2 (page 20) correlates some instructional implications for schools that use MLDs with each of the six skills that NETS emphasizes.

Table 2.2: Technology Standards for Students and Their Implications for Schools Using MLDs

NETS	Implications for Schools Using MLDs
Creativity and innovation	Use MLDs to generate original works. Create audio and visual presentations. Create animations and simulations.
Communication and collaboration	Contribute to a team and instantly publish with peers using multimedia.
Research and information fluency	Find, organize, and synthesize information obtained from a wide variety of sources.
Critical thinking, problem solving, and decision making	Investigate authentic problems and participate in activities to find solutions. Use MLDs to collect and analyze data to find solutions.
Digital citizenship	Practice digital safety and citizenship with MLDs. Self-advocate for personal lifelong learning.
Technology operations and concepts	Choose MLD applications appropriately, and adjust current knowledge to new and emerging technologies.

Leveraging Novelty

Novelty stimulates learning. Neurobiologists have known for some time that a novel environment or activity sparks exploration and learning (Jensen, 2008). Fun, different, unusual, odd, surprising, and even strange are characteristics that excite students about content and create opportunities to stimulate learning. Researchers have also long indicated that the human brain is naturally attracted to new information and that new information is important for stimulating learning. Brain researchers agree that to stimulate learning, the brain needs movement, humor, hydration, music, feedback, and novelty. Movement, laughter, and hydration assist in carrying oxygen to the brain. Music, timely feedback, and novelty provide inspiration and motivation, which also stimulate learning (Sousa, 2001). It does not take much for a mobile learning device to bring the "wow" factor of novelty and fun in the classroom. As a simple test, bring an iPad into the classroom and see how students respond.

Brain-based education says to be purposeful about instruction, since everything you do in your classroom has some effect on the brain. Eric Jensen (2008) identifies four teacher actions that will make cognitive miracles happen for students. First, to increase students' attention span, assign relevant instructional tasks. Second, develop students' processing skills by using games to enhance working memory and sequencing. This can be done by working with partners or in groups and solving problems by trial and error. Third and fourth, introduce these actions with focus and vigor. Jensen suggests that these are the hardest strategies to use when trying to boost brain function in students. The teacher needs to get students excited about the activities, and the activities must be incorporated on a frequent basis (Jensen, 2010).

I agree with Jensen. Getting students excited about learning is a challenge. Educators often use the novelty of technology to try to meet the challenge of engaging students. In fact, it has been my experience that student excitement is palpable when even just the possibility of using cell phones is mentioned.

However, as with any technology in the classroom, MLDs should not be used for the sake of novelty alone. The Institute for Global Education and Service-Learning (2010) reports that too much novelty for students can create distress; at the same time, too little novelty can foster boredom. By balancing the novelty of technology with good instruction, teachers can hook students into learning.

Making MLDs Instructionally Relevant

Most reviews of mobile technology in learning categorize the learning into specific content areas. For instance, a white paper might discuss the use of iPads in reading or science. On the other hand, Naismith et al. (2004) identified six broad theory-based categories of activities for using MLDs for learning. Although the identified themes are based upon previous existing theories of learning, the authors of this study sought to review new and emerging instructional practices that coincided with previous existing theories and practices.

The themed instructional activities in the Naismith study deal specifically with MLDs. Presenting these themed activities in an instructionally relevant context for teachers, it has to be done in tandem with instructional practices with which they are most familiar, for example, Robert Marzano's strategies—identifying similarities and differences; summarizing and notetaking; reinforcing effort and providing recognition, homework, and practice; nonlinguistic representation; cooperative learning; setting objectives; and providing feedback (Marzano, Pickering & Pollock, 2001).

The themed activities identified in the Naismith et al. (2004) study are broad-based, observable activities that students and teachers can do with MLDs. Marzano's strategies are instructional strategies that can be done with or without MLDs. Naismith's findings, in addition to research-based instructional strategies identified by Marzano, Pickering, and Pollock (2001), will serve as our base for this discussion. The Naismith et al. (2004) literature review was selected because it is more detailed and complex than other literature reviews. The instructional strategies suggested by Marzano, Pickering, and Pollock were selected because they are more widely adopted by school districts across the country than others.

The six themed mobile learning activities proposed by Naismith et al. (2004) are as follows:

1. Behaviorist activities

2. Constructivist activities

3. Situated learning

4. Collaborative learning

5. Informal and lifelong learning

6. Learning and teaching support

Table 2.3 (page 22) shows the relationship among Marzano's instructional strategies, 21st century learning skills, NETS skills, and Naismith's themed mobile learning activities. Let's look at these one by one in terms of the Marzano instructional strategies that best support them.

Behaviorist Activities

These types of activities promote learning as a change in the learners' observable actions (similar to B. F. Skinner's (1965) work of stimulus and response) and involve, for example, creating activities that utilize cell phones as clickers or polling devices. The strategies that best support behaviorist activities are summarizing and comparing similarities and differences (Marzano et al., 2001).

Behaviorist activities follow drill and feedback patterns. While they are not necessarily higher-order thinking activities, they allow teachers to check for understanding and to collect data on the progress of individual students. Nintendo DS and DSi chat functions, Twitter, backchanelling (using devices that are networked to hold a real-time online conversation during a live oral presentation), and websites like www.polleverywhere.com, www.wifitti.com, and www.textmarks.com are great for checking for understanding.

Activities of this nature that use mobile learning devices allow teachers to formatively assess students either via multiple-choice questions or free-text questions. The beauty of using MLDs is that they allow each student to respond anonymously, and the teacher is able to gather visual data, usually in the form of a graph, that conveys the thinking of the entire class. Students less apt to speak up during class discussions also benefit from activities that incorporate behaviorist activities. In many cases, the responses serve as a beginning to deeper conversations about the topic being studied.

Table 2.3: Relationships Among Instructional Strategies, 21st Century Learning Skills, and Mobile Learning Themed Activities

Instructional Strategies	Partnership for 21st Century Skills	NETS Skills	Themed Mobile Learning Activities
Cooperative learning	Creativity and innovation Communication and collaboration	Creativity and innovation Communication and collaboration Digital citizenship	Situated Collaborative
Summarizing	Critical thinking, problem solving, and decision making	Critical thinking, problem solving, and decision making Communication and collaboration Research and information fluency Digital citizenship	Behaviorist Constructivist Informal and lifelong learning Learning and teaching support
Comparing similarities and differences	Critical thinking, problem solving, and decision making	Critical thinking, problem solving, and decision making	Behaviorist Constructivist Informal and lifelong learning Learning and teaching support

Constructivist Activities

These activities give students a chance to learn in a real-world context with access to supporting tools (in many cases, the Internet). The constructivist activities align nicely with Marzano's summarizing and similarities and differences strategies. Students are often involved in situated learning with these types of activities (Naismith et al., 2004)—games in which the student is part of the simulation. Having students use an iPad, iPod touch, or netbook to participate in activities that utilize websites such as ClubPenguin, Webkinz, Gaiaonline, and Second Life gives them opportunities to interact with other students locally or around the globe in real-world situations.

Situated Learning

Students can use MLDs in environments such as museums and zoos—what's called "situated learning"—and thus actively participate in authentic learning environments. Situated learning is also enhanced by problem-based learning, in which students work in groups to solve a problem. Assessment is typically performance based. Situated learning is best supported by Marzano's cooperative learning instructional strategy. Science activities and experiments are great examples of situated learning—for example, students' participating in an archeological dig as part of a science unit or recording leaf measurements in a greenhouse. Situated learning activities allow for use of such small-group skills as communication, decision making, and conflict resolution (Naismith et al., 2004).

Collaborative Learning

Long gone is the traditional image of learning as a single teacher sharing her insight and wisdom with her students. Students expect to engage with each other to make sense of information and create meaning. Kids today are accustomed to doing this through exploration and experimentation. Generation text learns through meaningful conversations (often virtual); they reflect and evaluate almost nonstop. When you think about it, this process is also the way we as adults learn daily (Marzano, 2003; Vavoula, Sharples, Lonsdale, Rudman, & Meed, 2007).

Mobile learning and MLDs lend themselves perfectly to collaborative learning. Unless you are fortunate enough to have a one-to-one initiative for a particular mobile learning device, your students will end up sharing a device and working collaboratively in small groups. In fact, I highly recommend that teachers form students into groups initially for two reasons—instruction and management.

Instructionally, small groups just make sense. One of the key skills that the Partnership for 21st Century Learning identifies is collaboration (Partnership for 21st Century Skills, 2008). Working collaboratively using MLDs teaches higher-level thinking skills, builds oral communication skills, enhances self-management, addresses learning style differences, and gives students opportunities to build leadership skills.

Managing students while they are conducting activities with mobile learning devices is an important concern. By integrating collaborative learning with mobile learning devices, educators can promote student responsibility for learning, enhance self-management skills, and teach students how to criticize ideas, not people. Typically, when students are working collaboratively with MLDs, they are more active learners and tend to hold each other accountable for learning (Project Tomorrow, 2010).

Informal and Lifelong Learning

As opposed to the traditional stand-and-deliver method of teaching, which is often referred to as *formal* teaching, mobile learning is often referred to as *informal* because it can be done without constraints of time or place. Mobile learning devices can accompany students in everyday experiences and automatically become a source of valuable information that can assist with learning on demand (Elliott, 2006). Using devices spontaneously to conduct research and sift through information is characteristic of skills students will use in the workforce. The instructional strategies of summarizing and comparing similarities and differences are the most appropriate strategies to use with informal and lifelong activities.

Learning and Teaching Support

Mobile learning devices eliminate the need for learning and teaching support to occur in a specific time and space. For example, teachers can use an iPad to access school district student management systems to take attendance, record grades, and so on, regardless of time and place. Administrators can conduct walkthroughs, send information, and communicate with parents via text messaging—without being confined to their offices. Summarizing and comparing similarities and differences are instructional strategies that could be used during an MLD in-service for teachers and that align well with learning and teaching support activities.

Aligning Technology With Research-Based Instructional Strategies

An instructional strategy is simply a tool with which instruction can be delivered. Results will vary, and teachers have to determine the most effective instructional strategy to use to obtain the best results. When our teachers designed lessons and activities, we always kept research-based instructional practices in mind. As mentioned, we focused on three of Marzano et al.'s (2001) research-based instructional strategies—summarizing, note taking, and comparing similarities and differences. As we created and conducted lessons using MLDs, we noticed that students using the devices worked best when they were allowed to work in small groups. As a result, we added an additional strategy: cooperative learning. These four strategies helped us to create pedagogical focus when designing lessons and activities, particularly when we used cell phones. In addition, we selected these strategies according to their large effect sizes.

Table 2.4 contains a comprehensive list of learning opportunities for nine MLDs. You can see from the table that cell phones, iPads, iPod touches, and netbooks allow for the greatest versatility when engaging students in learning opportunities. This is primarily because those tools can access the Internet. Note that the list of MLDs in the chart is not exhaustive; many MLDs available for students to use are not addressed in this book.

Table 2.4: Learning Opportunities With MLDs

	Cell Phone	iPad	iPod touch	iPod	MP3	Nintendo DS or DSi	PSP	eReader	Netbook
Alerts	•	•	•	•		•	•		•
Assignments	•	•	•	•					•
Audio Blogging	•	•	•	•	•				•
Audio Recording	•	•		•	•		•		•
Augmented Reality	•	•		•				•	•
Calculating	•	•	•	•		•	•		•
Capture, Share, and Document Display (Uploading photos and video to social networking sites)	•	•	•	•		•			•
Checklists	•	•		•					•
Coaching or Mentoring	•	•		•	•	•	•	•	•
Contextualized Learning	•	•	•	•	•	•	•	•	•
Evaluation	•	•	•	•	•				•
Feedback	•	•		•		•			•
Game-Based Learning	•	•	•	•		•	•	•	•
Geo Blogging (Adding geographical identification to photos or text on websites)	•	•	•	•					•
Geo Exploration (Global positioning system—GPS)	•	•	•	•					•
Job Aid (On the job training)	•	•	•	•	•	•	•	•	•
Journaling	•	•		•	•	•	•		•
Just in Time	•	•	•	•	•	•	•	•	•
Location-Specific Field Guide	•	•		•					•

continued →

	Cell Phone	iPad	iPod touch	iPod	MP3	Nintendo DS or DSi	PSP	eReader	Netbook
Microblogging	●	●	●	●					●
Microlearning (getting short pieces of information from short blogs or tweets)	●	●		●	●	●	●	●	●
Note Taking	●	●		●		●			●
On-Demand Access	●	●		●	●	●	●	●	●
Organizing	●	●		●		●	●		●
Photo Blogging	●	●	●	●					●
Polling	●	●		●	●	●	●	●	●
Presentations	●	●		●	●		●		●
Problem-Based Learning	●	●		●	●	●	●	●	●
Procedures	●	●		●		●			●
Quizzes or Tests	●	●	●	●	●	●	●		●
References	●	●		●				●	●
Remembering	●	●		●		●	●		●
Reminders	●	●		●		●			●
Reporting	●	●	●	●					●
Reviewing	●	●	●	●	●	●	●		●
Simulating	●	●	●	●		●	●		●
Study Aids	●	●	●	●	●	●	●	●	●
Surveying	●	●		●					●
Transcribing	●	●	●	●	●				●
Translating	●	●	●	●	●	●	●	●	●
Updates	●	●	●	●		●	●		●
Video Recording	●	●	●	●		●			●
Writing	●	●		●	●	●	●	●	●

3

Mobile Technology Integration

When considering pedagogy when integrating mobile technology, we often omit purpose and process. This chapter proposes a framework that can be used to assist with the purpose and process of true integration of MLDs.

"I use PowerPoint to give notes, and we watch United Streaming Clips" is an all too familiar response when I ask educators how they incorporate technology with instruction. Of course, the trend now is to add, "I use my interactive whiteboard to show PowerPoints and United Streaming Clips."

I think educators misunderstand the difference between using technology and integrating technology. First, let's be clear about what technology integration is not. Integration is not scheduling the computer lab once to create content or devise a pretty graph that indicates the progress of students. Integration is also not letting students use web-based games that have no instructional merit. And technology integration is not using programs and software that are nothing more than electronic worksheets that are unrelated to the curriculum and have little instructional value or purpose.

Alan November (personal communication, August 10, 2010) is very concerned about the way we integrate technology in schools today and about the lack of purpose given when using technology to support instruction. In other words, too often we as educators fail to identify the reasons we use technology. When we don't clearly identify purposeful reasons for using technology, we run the risk of using technology just for the sake of using technology. Here are some of the comments I have heard in this regard:

> *"I don't teach 21st century skills because I don't have the time. I have to teach what's in the curriculum. My students get 21st century skills when they go on the computer at home."*

> *"21st century teaching means using technology every chance you get. All of my notes are in PowerPoint, and students can download the PowerPoints from my web page."*

"I use my SMART Board to help my students with 21st century learning. Kids really take to technology. I even have a few students who will get the SMART Board set up for me before I begin lessons."

"My students love to earn computer lab time. I take them periodically and let them go on Funbrain.com or AAmath.com. They love playing the games."

Finding purpose and connection to curriculum when integrating technology is challenging for educators in part because true integration of technology is hard to define.

What Is Technology Integration?

Technology integration is a habit of mind that is routine and transparent (TPACK, 2010). True technology integration happens spontaneously. It's just done, almost without students' realizing it. It happens when classroom teachers use technology to introduce lessons and units, reinforce what was taught, extend important concepts, enrich interesting topics, assess for content understanding, and remediate student mastery. Only classroom teachers can make integration happen. Administrators cannot mandate technology integration—they have to model it and give recognition when it is happening. Administrators can model technology integration when they hold schoolwide professional development, run instructional meetings, and communicate school activities and events to students, staff, and parents. For example, principals can use classroom response systems or "clickers" to gain consensus from their staff on specific topics. They can also create monthly YouTube-style videos to post on school websites that make the community aware of events taking place at their schools. Principals can also influence technology integration by conducting walk-throughs and identifying specific technology usage with written feedback to teachers.

True integration of technology happens in classrooms where technology is accessible and available for activities as they are initiated. True integration of technology happens when form supports function when the tools support the goals of the curriculum and assist students in reaching their instructional goals.

TPACK

The Technological Pedagogical Content Knowledge (TPACK) framework is a multifaceted framework that attempts to capture the essential knowledge that is required for teachers to integrate technology into their instruction (TPACK, 2010). Matt Koehler and Punya Mishra's (2006) ongoing research experiment utilizes a framework that involves a close relationship among three forms of knowledge—content, pedagogy, and technology—that educators should consider when designing technology integrated lessons and activities. Mishra and Koehler maintain that true technology integration takes place when there is an understanding and explicit negotiation of the relationships among these three components. Their framework further suggests that a teacher who is capable of using all these relationships possesses a kind of expertise that is considerably different from, and greater than, that of someone with knowledge of just one of them—for example, a content expert (a mathematician or historian), a technology expert (such as a computer scientist), or someone with pedagogical expertise (such as an experienced educator). Effective technology integration requires developing sensitivity to the relationship among all three of these components. The TPACK framework thus gives foundational and background knowledge for technology integration that is extremely helpful for educators.

Based on the required knowledge that the TPACK framework recommends is needed, this chapter suggests a concrete step-by-step planning model that educators can use when designing lessons and activities that integrate technology. Although this book focuses primarily on mobile learning devices, this model can be used for any form of technology integration.

The ICE Model

What steps do teachers take to create worthwhile, relevant, engaging, and rigorous lessons using mobile learning? A simple model called the investigate, create, and evaluate (ICE) model that I have developed can be used as a framework for:

- Creating mobile learning lessons

- Identifying the purpose of integrating selected technology

- Showing the relationship between technology and curriculum

- Showing connections to 21st century skills

Educators wishing to create mobile learning–integrated lessons and activities can follow the ICE model (table 3.2, page 31) to answer the following three questions:

1. What will students learn in reference to the curriculum?

2. What will students do with the technology to help them learn the curriculum?

3. What 21st century skills will the activity address?

Investigate

In answering the first question, what will students learn in reference to the curriculum, educators should acquire a curriculum guide (hopefully an electronic version) to identify goals, objectives, lesson plans, and assessments. For example, if a teacher wants to plan an activity that incorporates cell phones to help students identify angles as part of a geometry unit, he could use the curriculum guide to identify student outcomes, such as "Students will identify and define three different types of angles." Commonalities between instructional objectives and outcomes and 21st century skills can then be identified.

Although the form (type of mobile learning device) can be selected either before or after its instructional function (what the technology can do) is identified, I suggest selecting the function first, especially if you are planning to use cell phones. Because cell phone use in instructional settings is so controversial, it helps to be able to make these instructional connections first.

Create

When creating a lesson to meet the goals selected in the investigate stage, educators must identify both the specific, research-based instructional strategies and the technology to use and how to use it.

Hence, the second question asks, what will students do with the technology to help them learn the curriculum? Answering this question is a little more involved, as we have so many forms of mobile learning and other technologies from which to choose. An educational technology facilitator or technology integration specialist can assist educators in determining which MLD to use and what students will do with it.

For example, for the identifying angles activity, the teacher may decide the following: Students will use the camera function of a cell phone to take pictures of three different angles around school. The pictures will be sent to Photobucket.com via text message and be downloaded to create a PowerPoint presentation. The presentation will compare and contrast the three types of angles.

For instance, in our angles activity, the teacher may use the activity to intentionally reinforce the 21st century skill of collaboration. She chooses that skill because she plans to ask students to work in groups of three to take the pictures and then in groups of two to create the PowerPoint.

Evaluate

The third question (what 21st century skills will be addressed with the activity?) forces us to reflect on what 21st century skills are, and to evaluate how the activity will explicitly teach skills in the areas of creativity and innovation, critical thinking, communication, and collaboration. Any lesson must plan for evaluation of student learning. Because technology integration is rarely planned for, or assessed for its effectiveness, this question is probably the most important to answer to ensure instructional relevance for mobile learning devices.

Reverting back to the angles activity, the teacher may assess a student's contribution to the project with the use of a rubric that indicates all facets that should have been included in the finished product—the PowerPoint.

Table 3.1 summarizes the three critical questions that should be answered, as well as action steps that should be taken when planning for technology integrated lessons. The blank ICE model tool in Table 3.2 is an example of what teachers can use when planning technology integrated lessons.

Tables 3.1 and 3.2 can be downloaded from **go.solution-tree.com/technology** and may also be found in reproducible form on pages 33–34.

Device Management and Student Grouping

Two important considerations when integrating MLDs into instruction are management of the devices themselves and student grouping.

How do you manage mobile learning in the classroom? This is one of the questions that I am frequently asked when I talk to educators. As a result of these conversations and my own experience with teachers, I have compiled a list of suggested points to consider.

- **Guidelines and expectations.** I always stress the importance of setting guidelines and expectations about appropriateness prior to using any mobile learning device. Specific strategies for this are discussed in chapter 4 (page 35).

- **Classroom setup.** Mobile learning works best in an open environment. Having students in rows is not the best arrangement; neither is having MLDs isolated in the back of the classroom. I would recommend spreading the technology throughout the classroom so that there is truly an integrated feeling and the technology is part of the class environment.

- **Labeling MLDs.** Naming or numbering mobile learning devices will assist with directing students to devices with which they are familiar. I have had teachers assign students to a particular calculator, iPod touch, or laptop computer. This step can help when grouping for projects or if students are able to save work to different devices.

Table 3.1: ICE Model for Mobile Learning and Technology-Integrated Lesson Planning

	Investigate	Create	Evaluate
Critical Questions	What will students learn in reference to the curriculum?	What will students do with the technology that will help them learn the curriculum?	What 21st century skill(s) will the activity address?
Action Steps	Identify objectives to be taught from the curriculum.	Identify the mobile learning device. Create a purposeful, explicit activity or lesson plan. Select research-based instructional strategies. Define what students will do with the technology. Identify which 21st century skills—creativity and innovation, critical thinking, communication, and collaboration—that the activity will address.	Identify how you will assess content learning and degree of 21st century skills improvement.

Table 3.2: Technology Integration Planning Form

Form of Mobile Technology to Be Used:		
Investigate	**Create**	**Evaluate**
Learning Outcomes	**Student Actions**	**21st Century Skills Outcomes**
What students will learn as a result of implementing this technology	What students will do with the technology using research-based instructional strategies	Creativity and innovation Critical thinking Communication Collaboration

- **Visual directions.** It's helpful to post the directions for the activity as well as any password or website information posted so that students can refer to it as they move through the activities. You can also post directions for using specific applications and using external peripherals (for example, printers).

- **Support.** How will students ask for assistance? Having a protocol for asking for assistance is helpful when using mobile learning. Identify a few resident experts to assist with troubleshooting problems. Schools may have older students participate in a technology or audiovisual club that could help with a teacher-student workshop and serve as a source for trained experts on the mobile learning device that will be used.

- **Student movement.** If the MLDs are part of a learning station, students can rotate through groups after a certain time period. Actual or web-based virtual timers can be used. If working independently or in pairs, students can notify each other by an agreed-upon class sign that indicates they are ready for the next phase of the activity.

Student groupings should also be purposeful and planned. A variety of student groupings can work with MLDs.

- **Individual.** Working alone is effective during projects that involve writing or activities that require some level of research.

- **Paired.** Establish a culture of shared responsibility by having students work in groups of two or more. Directions for group activities should be clear and include job-specific tasks.

- **Small groups.** Keep these truly small. With MLDs, groups larger than four are not as effective. Screen size is a hindrance to larger groups unless planning is deliberate and purposeful.

- **Whole class.** When we think of mobile learning, we don't usually think of whole-class instruction. But during whole-class instructional strategies—for example, when introducing a lesson or bringing closure to an activity—an LCD projector or document camera can be quite helpful.

Lessons and activities involving mobile learning and other technology should be authentic and based upon real-world connections, and they should have a strong relationship to what students are interested in. The ICE model for integration is not intended to create "something else" for educators to do in addition to completing regular lesson plans. It is good instructional practice to plan purposefully. Planning for mobile learning is no different.

Principals can provide guidance and support for teachers as they plan to integrate technology into their curricula by providing opportunities for exploration and professional development. Setting up professional learning communities that are composed of teachers who are also interested in technology integration is a great way to provide support. Opportunities for teachers to get together to share resources and brainstorm ideas are also helpful in guiding teachers to do the things discussed in this chapter.

ICE Model for Mobile Learning and Technology-Integrated Lesson Planning

Use this form to formulate and answer the three initial questions and to plan your action steps.

	Investigate	Create	Evaluate
Critical Questions			
Action Steps			

Technology Integration Planning Form

Use this form to plan for the use of a specific technology in the classroom.

Form of mobile technology to be used:		
Investigate	**Create**	**Evaluate**
Student Outcomes	Student Actions	21st Century Skills Outcomes

4

Strategies for Getting Started

"Make sure you don't tell the other students that we're using cell phones in class. Everyone else will want to use them, too." This is what I told my seventh-grade pre-algebra students when we first started using cell phones in class. They assured me that they would not share the secret. Almost instantly, of course, word got around, and I quickly realized that I needed to leverage student excitement and curiosity.

The key to the success of any school program, especially when it comes to technology, is the support of the principal (Alan November, personal communication, August 10, 2010). Without it, any major initiative involving technology is going to involve a steep, uphill battle. This challenge is especially so because of the controversial nature of mobile learning devices in the school setting.

Once you obtain the principal's support, move on to implementing the following strategies:

- Establish a technology team.

- Consider existing policies.

- Establish guidelines.

- Generate excitement.

- Solicit buy-in.

- Take affordability into account.

- Consider access for all students.

- Think big, start small.

Establish a Technology Team

If you don't have a technology team, you should certainly form one. Its members will serve as cheerleaders for the mobile learning initiative. The team should be made up of a heterogeneous mixture of staff from different grade levels and content areas.

This advice holds true for districtwide technology committees as well. At one of the first meetings, identify the goals, mission, function, and purpose of the committee. Will you focus your initial efforts on a specific grade level, content, or instructional superstars? What MLD will you use? When identifying goals, will the committee focus on student achievement, motivation, homework completion, summative assessment test scores, or 21st century skills? After the committee decides on its goals, mission, function, and purpose, come to consensus on an approach that focuses on a tiered rollout.

Having a technology committee will help with keeping the implementation cycle moving in the right direction. This committee will also be able to serve as a resource for teachers when questions arise.

Consider Existing Policies

Are your school district's technology policies rigid or flexible? Most school board policies are written such that students are not allowed to bring mobile devices in school at all, much less bring them into the classroom. New York City schools ban students from bringing cell phones to school—period. Ironically, New York City participated in a project called The Million, sponsored by Verizon Wireless (Rahulioizm, 2008). In this project, one million students were given cell phones and earned talking minutes by coming to school daily, doing homework, and passing tests. In a YouTube video called *Million,* students talk about how excited they are about the project and how they improved their grades and their participation and behavior in class. These testaments are confirmed by school staff sharing data about student improvement as a result of the project. Yet even with all of this success, New York students are still not allowed to bring the very tools that garnered the excitement, motivation, and success into the classroom.

New York City, on the extreme end, conceivably has legitimate reasons to ban cell phones—stemming from problems with cheating, soliciting fights, and taking inappropriate photos and videos in locker rooms. There are certain instances where cell phones may not be the best instructional tool to use in certain environments. That being said, most states and school systems take a more lenient approach by allowing students to either bring these devices to school and stow them (turned off) in their lockers or to keep them on their person as long as they are turned off (Richtel & Stone, 2009).

When I was a principal, I welcomed students' mobile learning devices. They were allowed to use MP3 players at lunch and on the bus. The policy was that students could use them at appropriate times; however, they were responsible for them. Very seldom did we ever hear about a stolen iPod or MP3 player. Somehow, students keep track of their own MLDs.

School divisions and school boards are engaging in a robust dialogue about policies and procedures for mobile learning devices in schools (Hupp, 2009). I believe school officials are realizing the potential of MLDs slowly but surely and are trying to come up with a balance among student needs and wants and home, school, and division policies. Students, of course, want their phones; schools are apprehensive about disruption, cheating, and sexting; parents want their children to have cell phones for safety reasons; and school board members struggle with what they should support.

Although the vast majority of school systems still ban the use of cell phones and other mobile learning devices, allowing students to use cell phones during specific times of the day is a growing trend.

Establish Guidelines

Let's face it, once the decision to permit MLDs is made, the potential for students to use them inappropriately in school is there, and inevitably, will happen. This is one of the biggest concerns for educators. How should teachers deal with misuse? How should administrators deal with it?

To begin, punish the behavior and not the technology. The goal should be to change student behaviors just as you would with any other inappropriate behavior. If a student is cheating with a cheat sheet, you deliver a consequence for cheating. You don't take pen and paper away from the student forever.

Students have to be taught appropriate use. One of my former principals used to tell me, "Kipp, assume nothing and teach everything." When you teach students appropriate use of technology, they rise to meet expectations. This tendency is even more likely when students are allowed to assist with determining what appropriate usage is.

Just as many teachers do on the first day of school, students should be allowed to assist with creating acceptable use and classroom expectations for mobile learning devices. Basic classroom and school polices should address etiquette and manners, privacy, safety, and consequences for inappropriate use.

Etiquette and Manners

Have you ever stood in the checkout line in a store, waiting impatiently to pay for something, only to be further delayed by the customer in front of you texting or talking on a cell phone? or observed families dining out with the parents on their cell phones and their children playing with hand-held games—while eating? If you have not, I am almost certain you will soon. We have entered a culture where using mobile learning devices anytime and anywhere is acceptable.

When I taught, I always operated from the assume-nothing-and-teach-everything school of philosophy. If I wanted students to do something, I had to teach them. We can't assume that students inherently know proper etiquette and manners when using mobile devices, partly because adults violate the very rules we want students to follow. We have to teach students that talking on the phone while at the cash register of Subway is rude, especially when you are speaking loudly and everyone can hear your conversation. Leaving your ringer on in a restaurant is also rude. Teach children to hold conversations outside of public facilities and to turn their cell phones on vibrate in pubic settings. Teach them also that it is rude to wear earbuds and play handheld games during public gatherings when they should be paying attention.

Principals should encourage teachers to give students real-world scenarios, such as asking them to share how they should deal with cell phone use at movie theaters. Ultimately, the guide for how we address the use of MLDs in school should be common courtesy.

Privacy

The guidelines for recording should be clearly and specifically addressed. Students should not be allowed to record voice, still, or moving images of each other or of the teacher without permission. Students should certainly not post recordings online without permission.

A considerable amount of time should be spent discussing what is and what is not appropriate for online publication. Use this time to discuss school and district expectations, digital literacy, and especially digital footprints (the data trail that is left when any activity is conducted in a digital environment). When I was a principal, we taught students that any information that could be transmitted wirelessly could be traced back to the originator of the message. Whether that is a true statement or not is debatable. However, I have yet to have a student challenge me about it.

Safety

If you plan to use mobile learning devices that are capable of accessing the Internet, be sure to discuss safety first. We placed a lot of emphasis on cell phone safety before allowing students to use them in class. You may also consider having students complete an Internet safety quiz. The instructional technology person in your school or district should be able to assist you.

Once guidelines are set, post them around your school, and refer to them frequently. This will help to create a culture of appropriate use. If you have several teachers who are introducing MLDs, create a slideshow and share it, so that all students hear the same message.

Security

One of the great characteristics of mobile learning devices is their portability and size. Most MLDs can fit unobtrusively in a pocket. But precisely because of their portability, it is wise to have a plan in place to keep them from being lost or stolen. One of my teachers used an engraving tool to etch numbers on her classroom set of Nintendo DSs. When students used their own MLDs, she made sure that they had put their names on them. Many MLDs have a security feature on them so that people have to enter some sort of code before they can use them. If students are using their personal MLDs, ask them to create a security code for their devices.

Classroom sets of mobile learning devices should be clearly marked, and a check-out system should be devised. You can use a simple number-name system. For example, Jaquan always has the number 7 iPod touch. Teachers should always build in time to check the devices in and out.

Consequences

I have had many conversations with administrators about the problems they face when students bring mobile learning devices to school. Many say they spend a lot of time on this issue—especially dealing with cell phones. My impulse, again, is to punish the behavior and not the technology. No matter how much you try, you can't get the technology to go away; however, you can work toward making inappropriate behaviors go away. When we go into a theater or courtroom, we are taught appropriate cell phone etiquette—signs politely ask us not to use our cell phones, and for the most part, we comply.

That is not the case in schools. With MLDs, the typical misbehavior is sending or receiving text messages during class. Educators often become incredibly irritated by this. School policies dealing with this misbehavior vary, ranging from "please turn it off" all the way to suspension. A tiered approach should be taken. In the event a student is caught texting (passing notes 21st century style), a teacher should respond as if the student were passing a paper note and either ask him to turn the phone off or keep the phone for him until the end of class. I also recommend having a conversation with the student about staying focused on classroom instruction, participating in class, and not being distracted. If the teacher makes a big deal about it, it will become a big deal.

Here is a sample tiered system of consequences:

1. Give a verbal warning.

2. Confiscate the cell phone until the end of the day.

3. Call the student's home.

Generate Excitement

The moment you mention that you are interested in doing a mobile learning project, you will pique the interest of teachers and students alike. Having students complete a simple survey using Google Docs or another survey tool like Survey Monkey that asks them what kinds of technology they have will generate a certain buzz around your school. A survey that was used in York County School Division in Yorktown, Virgina, can be downloaded at **go.solution-tree .com/21stcenturylearning**; it may also be found in reproducible form on page 44. Use the data gathered from the survey to assist in determining the type of MLD that your technology team will pursue. The survey should help to determine how many students in your school own MLDs. If they are using cell phones, the survey will identify what peripherals they have on their phones and what kind of service they have (texting and talking minutes, for example).

Many students are unaware of their cell phone plans. I recommend having the student and parent(s) complete the survey together and sign the acceptable use policy. You want to avoid having angry parents coming to your office saying that their cell phone bill is astronomical because of a classroom activity. When my son was in eighth grade, I noticed he was spending a great deal of time talking to a young lady on the telephone. I casually asked him whether the young lady had Verizon. I wanted to be sure that she was in his "circle." He assured me that she did. Well, he was wrong, and my Verizon bill was over $500!

A great cafeteria conversation for you as the principal is to informally survey your students to see how many text messages they send in a month. You will be amazed to find that most students average three to four thousand messages monthly.

Solicit Buy-In

Most teachers and parents will be excited about your plan to implement mobile learning devices in your school. Others will regard it skeptically. Although they make up the minority, there are parents who will absolutely not want their children to use MLDs at school—especially cell phones. You will need to increase your stakeholders before implementing an MLD project. Following are some suggestions for creating buy-in.

To address the concerns of skeptics, you have to be purposeful with how you roll out the project. Start by generating some conversation with your staff. I began by going directly to certain staff that I knew would take the idea of the mobile learning project and develop it into a meaningful instructional practice. By doing this, I was able to build capacity. Together we crafted a process for presenting the project to our students, parents, central administrative staff, and the community.

Our teachers sent a letter home to explain what we were doing and to request parent permission. Students are very excited about being able to share this new activity at home. I don't think any of my students forgot to bring their permission slip from home. In addition, the letters requested information on whether students were able to send or receive text messages or access the Internet with their cell phones (Rogers, 2009a). The letters you and your staff send home should do the following:

- Explain the instructional unit, the related objectives, and how the unit ties into state standards.

- Explain that there will be planned alternate assignments for students who do not own their own MLD (particularly cell phones).

- Describe any associated costs.

- Give contact information for those who want to know more or who have questions.

In addition to the parental permission form, I recommend sending home a separate copy of the acceptable use policy. The form and policy may be downloaded from **go.solution-tree .com/technology** and can be found in reproducible form on pages 45 and 46.

Take Affordability Into Account

As you design activities, you have to keep cost in mind. Several functions do not incur any cost. However, if you are using text messaging or a multimedia messaging service, you need to be aware of what charges these activities incur. While most of the activities and websites mentioned in this book are free, some are being beta tested and will eventually end up costing money. The good news is that lots of free websites have the same functions as those that are fee based.

You will probably find through surveying your students that most have unlimited text messaging packages, but their talking minutes are many times limited. For that reason, I discouraged use during school hours of services that did not have 1–800 numbers or were not toll free. Many students had plans that allowed them to make regular calls after 7:00 p.m. without additional cost, and some activities could be done using a regular landline phone.

Consider Access for All Students

The question of what to do with students who don't have a Nintendo DS, iPod, or cell phone always comes up. The conversation centers around their feeling inadequate or bad because they don't have their own device. It's true, not all kids have these devices; however, many have access at home, and this is why a survey of your students will come in handy. Several strategies can be used if you don't have a one-to-one mobile learning initiative at your school.

One strategy is to use one device as part of a differentiated small-group activity. Elementary students will do very well in groups of two or three using one device. Middle and high school students will respond similarly. You can also use a few devices and place students in groups.

Another option is to consider obtaining used devices. For example, in many instances you will find that students will either own or have access to handheld game systems like the Nintendo DS. In May of 2009, Nintendo released a report saying that one in ten people owned a Nintendo DS in the United States (Plunkett, 2009). Not one out of ten gamers, one out of ten people. Keep in mind that number does not include people who have upgraded to more modern versions of the gaming system. To give it some perspective, my family has two Nintendo DSs. Both my daughter and son have one. My son is actually on his second one, as I spilled a drink on his and replaced it. In Japan, the numbers are even greater. Over 20 percent of the population have a Nintendo DS! I assure you, your students can obtain one if you wish to use it in the classroom.

As newer generations of MLDs hit the market, consumers want to replace their current devices with the newer models. The iPod has had several different generations. So have Nintendo and the Portable Play Station. While it's great to have the latest in technology, the truth is, you can conduct a great lesson using earlier generations of technology tools. In fact, I highly recommend it. For example, the major differences between the Nintendo DS, and the Nintendo DSi are the camera function and some Wi-Fi options. The regular Nintendo DS works just fine for instructional purposes without the camera feature, it is more accessible to students, and the cost is significantly lower. A used Nintendo DSs can be purchased for about fifty dollars from sites like Craig's List, and a new one can be purchased for as little as eighty dollars from Internet sites like Amazon.com. Finding other MLD items on these websites can save a great deal of money. Teachers have told me that when they went into their local game stop, spoke with a manager, and shared their proposal, they were able to purchase used handheld gaming systems for an extremely reduced price.

When I first began incorporating cell phones, I had an old Motorola Razor that I allowed students to use in center activities. Those models were the best because of their ease of use of the peripherals. I also asked some of my staff to donate old cell phones they had not turned in. Tell your local mobile service providers about your project. They are usually very generous with donating used cell phones for instructional usage. One company gave a teacher a set of ten of the same model cell phone, which was tremendously helpful for planning instruction using MLDs.

There are also grants available for studying mobile learning in instructional settings. Because the concept is still relatively new, with endless possibilities, more and more companies are exploring it. Verizon Wireless awarded two elementary schools in Indiana grants to incorporate mobile learning tools in class. During my last year as a principal, I partnered with the Mobile Learning Network, which loaned us a set of cell phones with Internet access for about a month. We conducted a project that utilized social networking and research using cell phones.

Limited Use

At one forward-thinking Nebraska school, students are allowed to use cell phones and other mobile learning devices during the fifth hour, which is their lunch period (Baker, 2009). Many school divisions are following suit and coming up with policies like the following (Millard Public Schools, 2010):

> Cell phones and other electronic devices may be used during passing periods and lunch. Usage in classrooms is up to the discretion of each individual teacher. Students need to be aware of their teacher's expectations regarding these electronic devices. Failure to comply with appropriate electronic device etiquette may result in disciplinary action. If a student is using a cell phone or electronic device in violation of school or classroom rules, the student will have the item confiscated and turned in to the security desk.

> Confiscated cell phones and other electronic devices may be picked up the following day by students at the security desk. On the day of confiscation, the student's parent/guardian may retrieve the device at the end of the school day at the security desk unless the object seized is dangerous, contrary to law or school policy, or has been turned over to legal authorities. Students need not ask for their cell phones or other electronic devices after school on the day of confiscation because they will not be returned. Electronic items will be returned to the student or parent/guardian at the discretion of the administration. Failure to give the cell phone or other electronic device to a staff member upon request will be considered insubordination resulting in disciplinary action. Repeated infractions of the cellular phone or other electronic device guidelines will result in escalated consequences.

A general version of this policy can be found at **go.solution-tree.com/technology** and in reproducible form on page 43.

Think Big, Start Small

Once guidelines and access have been established, the fun part begins—planning activities. Keep them extremely simple in the beginning. Remember, the focus should be on good instruction first and technology second. Create a getting-familiar-with-your-phone activity. For example, ask students to enter their homework in the notes section of the phone or to use the calculator function to complete an activity. One of my teachers had her students brainstorm all the instructional activities that could be accomplished using the cell phone. This activity can be repeated with the other mobile learning devices.

Sample Cell Phone Policy

Cell phones and other electronic devices may be used during passing periods and lunch. Usage in classrooms is up to the discretion of each individual teacher. Students need to be aware of their teacher's expectations regarding these electronic devices. Failure to comply with appropriate electronic device etiquette may result in disciplinary action. If a student is using a cell phone or electronic device in violation of school or classroom rules, the student will have the item confiscated and turned in to the security desk.

Confiscated cell phones and other electronic devices may be picked up the following day by students at the security desk. On the day of confiscation, the student's parent or guardian may retrieve the device at the end of the school day at the security desk unless the object seized is dangerous, contrary to law or school policy, or has been turned over to legal authorities. Students need not ask for their cell phones or other electronic devices after school on the day of confiscation because they will not be returned. Electronic items will be returned to the student, parent, or guardian at the discretion of the administration. Failure to give the cell phone or other electronic device to a staff member upon request will be considered insubordination resulting in disciplinary action. Repeated infractions of the cell phone or other electronic device guidelines will result in escalated consequences.

Class Survey of Mobile Learning Device Use and Availability

Name _____

1. Do you own a cell phone?   ☐ Yes   ☐ No

2. What features do you have on your cell phone? (check all that apply)

   ☐ Calculator   ☐ Tip Calculator   ☐ Camera

   ☐ Video Camera   ☐ Stop Watch   ☐ Alarm

   ☐ Internet   ☐ Text Messaging   ☐ Multimedia Messaging

   ☐ Address Book   ☐ Blue Tooth   ☐ Voice Recorder

   ☐ Memo Pad   ☐ Other _____   ☐ Other _____

3. How many text messages are you allowed to use per month?

   _____

4. How many cell phone talking minutes can you use per month?

   _____

5. What cell phone features do you use most often?

   _____

   _____

6. How do you feel about being able to use your cell phone in class to learn?

   _____

   _____

   _____

Sample Policy on Acceptable Use of Cell Phones in Class

Name _____

1. Students will use their cell phones to only complete assignments that are related to the instructional lesson.

2. Students will keep cell phones turned off or left in lockers when they are not being used for instructional purposes in class.

3. Students will only send text messages, pictures, or video messages to others outside of the classroom with permission and directions from the teacher.

4. Students will not record still or moving images or voices of students or the teacher without permission from the teacher.

5. Students will not post recordings of still or moving images or voice recordings of students or the teacher online without their permission.

6. Students will practice Internet safety with online resources.

7. Students will post only appropriate text, audio, and visual media to online websites.

- -

I _____understand that violation of our class acceptable cell phone use policy may result in my not being able to participate in additional class activities that involve using the cell phone. I also understand that I may receive disciplinary consequences for violating school board policies regarding cyberbullying.

I _____ have gone over the policy on acceptable use of cell phones in class with my child and agree to allow my child to participate.

_____
Parent's signature

_____
Student's signature

_____
Teacher's signature

Sample Letter to Families Regarding Cell Phone Use in Class

Dear Family,

As part of 21st century learning, students in our class will be participating in an instructional unit in which they will be allowed to use their cell phones in class. Students who have cell phones will be able to use the following features:

- Calculator

- Stopwatch

- Camera and/or video

- Text messaging (if available)

Acceptable use of cell phones during classroom use is expected. Our policy on acceptable use of cell phones in class is attached. Please go over the policy with your child, sign, and return.

We are looking forward to doing some exciting activities using the cell phone in class that will enhance student understanding of district, state, and national standards. If you have questions, please do not hesitate to contact me at _____.

Sincerely,

- -

My child _____,

☐ has my permission to use the text messaging feature on his/her cell phone.

☐ has my permission to use limited text messaging on his/her cell phone and should not go over _____ [number] sent/received text messages.

☐ will not be able to use the text messaging feature on his/her cell phone.

We have discussed the acceptable classroom use of the cell phone.

_____

Parent signature

_____

Student signature

_____

Parent Contact Number

Nine Common MLDs That Support Instruction

Many school districts across the country are challenged fiscally, and therefore, the availability of digital and video cameras, MP3 players, and even computers is not as widespread as we would like. However, the ubiquity of mobile learning devices—especially student-owned devices—allows the use of relatively expensive technology with a large number of students (Teaching Today, n.d.). There are many ways that MLDs can be used to collect data, record, and create content. As we pointed out earlier, even older devices, if they can perform these functions, can be useful in classroom instruction.

This chapter describes activities and lessons for nine devices. Detailed lesson plans using each of the nine devices can be downloaded from **go.solution-tree.com/technology** and photocopied from pages 57 to 65.

Cell Phones

The possibilities for using cell phones are limited only by your creativity and the available peripherals. The typical cell phone's peripherals include the following:

- Calendar

- Notepad

- Calculator

- Stopwatch

- Alarm

- Voice recorder

- MP3 player

- Camera

- Video camera

- SMS text messaging

- MMS

- Telephone

- Internet

In my first book, *Mobile Learning Using Cell Phones: Activities for the Classroom* (Rogers, 2009b), I identified three levels of instructional activities involving cell phones. Level 1 activities can be completed without having active service. These activities involve the calendar, calculator, notepad, stopwatch, voice recorder, and MP3 player. Level 2 activities require the use of SMS text messaging and web 2.0 tools that interact with SMS text messaging. Sites such as www.polleverywhere.com, www.wiffiti.com, and www.twitter.com are able to interact with cell phones and text messaging. Level 3 activities are activities that involve using both SMS and MMS text messaging features in conjunction with mobile-to-web websites.

Table 5.1 shows a list of possible activities for each of these cell phone functions. This list is by no means exhaustive and should serve as a springboard for teachers to generate ideas for additional lessons, projects, and activities. Visit **go.solution-tree.com/technology** to download the Cell Phone Calculator Lesson Plan, or go to page 57 to find this lesson plan in reproducible form.

MP3 Players

MP3 players have been around since the "ListenUp" player appeared in 1996. They were initially dubbed digital audio players and shortly morphed into portable media players. Most mobile learning devices have some sort of MP3 player on them (Elliott, 2006). Typically, cell phones now include an MP3 player, so there is no need to buy a separate one. Most MP3 players allow the user to create and listen to recordings (podcasts). Students can use MP3 players to listen to books, stories, and poetry. They can also record their own projects and share them with classmates.

Table 5.2 (page 50) shows a list of possible activities using the MP3. Visit **go.solution-tree.com /technology** to download the MP3 Podcast Poetry Lesson Plan, or go to page 58, where you will find this lesson plan in reproducible form.

iPod

The iPod is a portable media player designed by Apple Inc. It was launched in October of 2001. Since then, there have been several generations of iPods, all with similar attributes. iPods are unique in that they not only allow the user to listen to and record audio files, but also allow viewing of video and games. iPods can be used to assist language learning by acting as digital voice recorders or camcorders to conduct interviews and to make audiovisual tours in museums. For example, English learners can create presentations about their communities and use the iPod voice recorder to create an audio recording in English or Spanish to share with other students.

Table 5.1: Cell Phone Activity Ideas

Function	Sample Lesson and Activity Ideas	Sample Resources
Calculator	• Make calculations in all contents.	
Calendar	• Record homework assignments. • Set alarms when projects are due.	Google Calendar
Notepad	• Record simple notes in class.	
Stopwatch	• Record timed activities.	
MP3 player	• Create audio stories. • Listen to audio books and podcasts. • Analyze musical poetry.	Audacity, GarageBand
Voice recorder	• Record conversations in world languages. • Record reading. • Record practice on instruments. • Record interviews. • Audioblog.	GarageBand, Audacity
Short messaging service (SMS) text messaging (using mobile-to-web and web-to-mobile sites)	• Use Google SMS as a dictionary, translator, and research tool. • Use as a polling device. • Use for back channel discussions. • Use to post written responses. • Use for flashcard reviews.	Google SMS, Polleverywhere, Gabcast, Blogger, Photobucket, Twitter, Blogger, Facebook, Rememberthemilk
Camera	• Create photo stories. • Use for data collection (for example, at zoos and museums). • Create clay and paper animation. • Use for compare-and-contrast activities. • Create visual representations of writing activities. • Use for photoblogging.	Photobucket.com, Flickr, animoto, PowerPoint, iMovie, Moviemaker, iPhoto, Blogger, Twitter, Facebook
Video camera	• Create infomercials. • Create how-to videos. • Create public service announcements. • Do i-reporting (public journalism—sharing photos and video of news events as they happen).	Photobucket, iMovie, Moviemaker
Multimedia messaging service (MMS) (using mobile-to-web and web-to-mobile sites)	• Post 1,000-character writings to blogs. • Do photoblogging. • Do video blogging. • Watch multimedia videos. • Create multimedia digital stories.	Blogger, Photobucket, Animoto, Twitter, Facebook
Internet or web browser	• Conduct research. • Watch instructional videos. • Play educational games.	Google, YouTube, AAmath

Table 5.2: iPod/MP3 Player Activity Ideas

Function	Sample Lesson and Activity Ideas	Sample Resources
iPod/MP3 player	• Create audio stories. • Create or listen to audio books and podcasts. • Analyze musical poetry. • Record reading samples. • Record field trips and other life experiences. • Record and listen to interviews. • Develop a script, and record a dramatized version of the script. • Record instrument practice. • Listen to and record letter sounds. • Listen to pronunciation of spelling words and vocabulary. • Record fluency. • Create an oral history project. • Listen to world language vocabulary and conversations. • Give audio spelling tests. • Listen to directions for learning center work. • Record poetry and short story readings for audio blogs. • Download study guides. • Use a National Public Radio podcast to start a Socratic seminar. • Create studycasts. • Ask students to take an audio test. • Give instructions. • Take audio notes.	GarageBand, Audacity
Images	• Use photos to generate discussion. • Promote creativity for a writing activity. • Give visual representation to a poem or science concept. • Create PowerPoint notes (jpeg images). • Create maps and diagrams. • Give writing prompts.	
Video player	• Create video podcasts. • Create public service announcements.	

Table 5.2 also shows a list of possible activities using the iPod. Visit **go.solution-tree.com/technology** to download the iPod Electronic Lab Report Lesson Plan, or go to page 59, where you will find this lesson plan in reproducible form.

iPod touch

The iPod touch can be used for learning and instructional purposes in six different ways: applications, Internet, videos, ebooks, slideshows, and podcasts. The iPod touch is probably best known for its multimedia functionality. Teachers and students can create audio and video podcasts and listen to MP3 files. There are literally thousands of applications available for the iPod touch, such as a graphing calculator, a science lab timer, world globe, and much more. The ways in which educators can apply this tool to education are almost limitless.

Table 5.3 shows a list of possible activities using the iPod touch. Visit **go.solution-tree.com /technology** to download the iPod touch Vocabulary Study Lesson Plan, or go to page 60, where you will find this lesson in reproducible form.

Table 5.3: iPod Touch Activity Ideas

Function	Sample Lesson and Activity Ideas	Sample Resources
Calculator	• Make calculations in all contents.	
Calendar	• Record homework assignments. • Set alarms when projects are due.	Google Calendar
Notepad	• Record simple notes in class.	
Stopwatch	• Record timed activities.	Any stopwatch app
MP3 player	• Create audio stories. • Listen to audio books and podcasts. • Analyze musical poetry.	iTunes, GarageBand
Voice recorder	• Record conversations in world languages. • Record reading. • Record practice on instruments. • Record interviews. • Do audioblogging. • Record lectures. • Record prewriting information.	GarageBand, Audacity
Slideshows	• View and create slideshows.	
eBooks	• Read and share ebooks.	eReader app
Applications	• Use applications to reinforce concepts in all content. • Use as a behavioral incentive.	
Videos	• Use a YouTube or TeacherTube clip to give inspiration for writing.	
Internet or web browser	• Conduct research. • Play instructional games.	

The iPod touch also allows for a portable Internet connection so that students can do research, access web resources, and collect data on the go. Most things that can be done on a regular computer can be adapted to a mobile platform. Along with Internet access, the iPod touch allows the user to access and play videos from the web. There are many educational videos available for students, ranging from Discovery Education's *United Streaming* to math simulations. Teachers and students can also create their own videos, which can be synched and viewed on an iPod touch, to enhance the curriculum.

eBook readers are also available on the iPod touch. Teachers can download and use ebooks in a similar manner to regular books to enhance reading skills and to promote reading fluency. The benefits of having books downloaded as ebooks are cost over time and limitless accessibility.

The iPod touch also has the ability to cater to different learning styles. Slideshows can easily be created on an Apple computer and synched to an iPod touch.

iPad

Apple advertises the iPad as "magical." I would have to agree. I mention earlier that the brain responds to novelty. I have yet to hand someone my iPad who is not amazed by what it can do. The iPad has functional qualities comparable to that of a computer. The applications, audio recording, Internet browsing, and publishing capabilities make this device a wonderful tool for educators to use in the classroom. Students can conduct research, post comments on blogs, collaborate by writing on Google Docs, or create multimedia-based presentations.

Table 5.4 shows a list of possible activities using the iPad. Visit **go.solution-tree.com/technology** to download the iPad Current Events Jigsaw Lesson Plan, or go to page 61, where you will find this lesson plan in reproducible form.

Table 5.4: iPad Activity Ideas

Function	Sample Lesson and Activity Ideas	Sample Resources
eReader	• Read books. • Ask students to read in small guided-reading groups. • Ask students to summarize or compare and contrast select readings.	
Calendar	• Record homework assignments. • Set alarms when projects are due.	
Word processor	• Create documents.	Pages
Presentation tools	• Create slideshow presentations.	Keynote
Special applications	• Use multimedia textbook applications. • Use second language applications. • Access newspapers.	
MP3 player	• Create audio stories. • Listen to audio books and podcasts. • Analyze musical poetry.	iTunes
Video player	• Record and play video.	
Audio recorder	• Create podcasts.	
Internet or web browser	• Conduct research. • Play instructional games.	

Nintendo DS, DSi, and DS 3000

The Nintendo handheld family boasts a good amount of educational games with promises for more advanced and complex titles. Educators can use the DS and its family of devices to play educational games, check for understanding, and work with students in small groups to reinforce instruction and create animated stories. The DS newer models have camera and music player capabilities that make enhancing high-yield instructional strategies even more exciting.

Table 5.5 shows a list of possible activities using the Nintendo DS. Visit **go.solution-tree.com/technology** to download the Nintendo DS Pictochat Math Lesson Plan, or go to page 62, where you will find this lesson in reproducible form.

Table 5.5: Nintendo DS or DSi Activity Ideas

Function	Sample Lesson and Activity Ideas	Sample Resources
Calendar	• Record homework assignments. • Set alarms when projects are due.	
Pictochat	• Use as a back channel during classroom discussions. • Use in small groups as a mini-whiteboard for teacher-student feedback. • Assign small groups to different chat rooms, and give them math problems to solve. • During reading, ask students to ask questions about the reading to members of the chat room. • Use to administer spelling or vocabulary tests. • Use with Socratic seminars. • Practice math, language, and grammar skills. • Practice penmanship. • Create animated stories.	
Recorder	• Create recordings of reading assignments. • Create recordings for podcasts.	
Educational games	• Use various content games as part of small-group learning activities. • Use for timed-math activities. • Use for vocabulary activities. • Use for counting money.	
Camera	• Create images to accompany written assignments. • Take photos of different leaf types. • Create a slideshow explaining steps of a science experiment.	
Internet or web browser	• Conduct research. • Play instructional games.	

Sony PSP

The Sony PSP is a more complex handheld gaming system. The instructional possibilities are such that students can use the music player, camera functionalities (which are integrated on newer models or can be added as an attachment on older models), video player functionalities, calendar, eReader, and web browser. Although Internet browser functionality is lacking, students who do not have full computers at home can complete simple research projects that utilize the Internet. Students can also create videos and podcasts and then download them to a PSP for later use.

Table 5.6 shows a list of possible activities using the Sony PSP. Visit **go.solution-tree.com /technology** to download the Sony PSP Vocabulary Book Lesson Plan, or go to page 63 to find this lesson plan in reproducible form.

Table 5.6: Sony PSP, PSP 3000, or PSP Go Activity Ideas

Function	Sample Lesson and Activity Ideas	Sample Resources
Calendar	• Record homework assignments. • Set alarms when projects are due.	
eBook reader	• Use book readers to read ebooks. • Read PDF files.	psp.manybooks.net
Photos viewer	• Use photos as a writing prompt. • View PowerPoint notes. • View maps and diagrams.	
Camera (PSP Go)	• Take photos of content. • Create slideshows. • Record visual data.	
MP3 player	• See MP3 player activities, page 50. • Create audio stories. • Listen to audio books and podcasts. • Analyze musical poetry.	iTunes, GarageBand
Video player	• See video player activities.	
Internet or Web browser	• Conduct research. • Play instructional games.	

eReader

I have yet to run into an educator who has an eReader who does not love it. The beauty of using this device in the classroom is that you can use a few eReaders with a large number of students. Having dictionaries already built into some of the eReaders is an advantage when building student vocabulary. Teachers can also use the eReaders to teach annotation and summarizing in literature circles and center activities. This tool is the perfect device to use with reluctant readers because students can focus on one page at a time, adjust font size, and define unfamiliar words without having to use a dictionary.

Table 5.7 shows a list of possible activities using the eReader. Visit **go.solution-tree.com /technology** to download the eReader (iPad) iBook Literature Circles Lesson Plan, or go to page 64, where you will find this lesson in reproducible form.

Table 5.7: eReader Activity Ideas

Function	Sample Lesson and Activity Ideas	Sample Resources
MP3 player	• Listen to audio books. • Listen to podcasts. • Listen to music while reading.	
eReader	• Read books. • Ask students to read in small guided-reading groups. • Form literature circles. • Hold round-table reading discussions.	
Internet or web browser	• Conduct research. • Play instructional games.	

Netbook

Netbooks allow much of the same versatility as traditional laptops when it comes to instruction. As a result of their portability, size, and long battery life, the netbook is ideal for the classroom setting. Additionally, netbooks are a cost-effective solution for increasing the computer-to-student ratio in schools. Teachers can use netbooks to create assignments that allow students to read and conduct research, write and publish original documents, create works of art, and contribute comments on their peer's work.

Table 5.8 shows possible activities using netbooks. Visit **go.solution-tree.com/technology** to download the Netbook Glogster Movie Poster Lesson Plan, or go to page 65, where you will find this lesson in reproducible form.

Table 5.8: Netbook Activity Ideas

Function	Sample Lesson and Activity Ideas	Sample Resources
Research	• Conduct research individually or in groups.	
Back channel	• Ask students to participate in back-channel discussions.	
Web cam	• Maintain a video diary. • Create a commercial or host a web TV show. • Use SKYPE to communicate with students in other locations. • Do role-playing activities. • Conduct interviews.	
Recording data	• Create a digital archive. • Do peer assessment assignments using commenting and voice threads.	

continued →

Function	Sample Lesson and Activity Ideas	Sample Resources
Special programs	• Use multimedia textbook applications to create photo stories, movies, music, podcasts, and videocasts.	
MP3 player	• Create audio stories. • Listen to audio books and podcasts. • Analyze musical poetry.	iTunes, GarageBand
Video player	• Record and play video.	
Recorder	• Podcasting	
Internet or web browser	• Conduct research. • Play educational games. • Write and maintain a blog or wiki.	

Summing Up

Much like the devices themselves, the manner in which a teacher uses any device is going to be varied. Many of the mobile learning devices can be used for word processing, conducting research, reading electronic books, and assessing students in all content areas. Students can also learn new skills and languages at times that are most convenient for them. What teachers choose to do is ultimately dependent upon what tools they have access to. This chapter merely scratches the surface of the possibilities of these nine MLDs.

Cell Phone Calculator Lesson Plan

Content Area: Math/Teen Living

Grade Levels: 6–8

Features and Materials: Calculator function, computer with Internet access, sample printed restaurant menus

ISTE Standards: Research and Information Fluency (3b)

21st Century Skills: Communication, collaboration, critical thinking

Activity Overview

In this activity, students will be given a virtual allowance of $300 to shop online. Students will be asked to visit websites of retail stores and decide on what merchandise to spend their money. The students will also be given virtual discount coupons to use for shopping. Students will participate in a class contest to spend all of their money and come closest to $300 without going over (including their discounted items and taxes).

Procedure

1. Place students in groups of two. Tell students they have $300 to spend. Tell students that they also have three discount coupons: one for 10% off of one item, one for 15% off of one item, and one for 25 percent off of one item.

2. Ask students to shop online to spend their money. Students should record the cost of the items they purchase in their cell phone notepads. Ask students to use their calculators to find the total of their purchases including taxes and after discounts.

3. Ask students to create a receipt for their purchases as an assessment of the activity.

4. The group that comes the closest to spending the $300 wins the shopping challenge.

Extension

1. Ask students to purchase a car and calculate interest over time.

2. Ask students to use a credit card to make the purchase and add 18% (annual interest rate) to the total bill. Engage students in a discussion about the cost of credit and annual interest rates.

MP3 Podcast Poetry Lesson Plan

Content Area: Language Arts/All Contents

Grade Levels: 4–12

Features and Materials: MP3 player, Audacity, or GarageBand

ISTE Standards: Creativity and Innovation (1a,1b), Technology Operations and Concepts (6a, 6b)

21st Century Skills: Communication, collaboration, creativity, and innovation

Activity Overview

In this activity, students will be given an opportunity to use their favorite song as inspiration to create and record a podcast of an original poem that is a spinoff of their favorite song. The students will then download each other's poems and identify several elements of poetry within each poem.

Procedure

1. Place students in groups of two or three. Have the group decide on a song to use for the activity. Students should work together to write the poem. The poem should be a continuation of the song, a response to the song, or a parody of the song.

2. Ask students to create a plan for their podcast. The plan should specify which student will read the poem and any music that will be used before, during, or after the podcast.

3. The reader should practice reading the poem to other students in the group. Have the students record the poem using Audacity or GarageBand (or any available digital audio recording software).

4. Ask students to publish the podcasts and upload them to a class website for other students in the class to be able to download to an MP3 player.

5. Ask students to download any two podcasts to their MP3 players and listen to them.

6. Ask students to identify any of the following elements of poetry: figurative language, rhyme, alliteration, and onomatopoeia, as well as any vivid words used in the poem.

Extension

Have a student or another staff member record several famous poems on an MP3 player, and use the MP3 player as part of a center activity. Ask students to compare and contrast two recorded poems on a Venn diagram.

iPod Electronic Lab Report Lesson Plan

Content Area: Science

Grade Levels: 4–12

Features and Materials: GarageBand, iMovie, cell phone camera or digital camera, and Photobucket .com

ISTE Standards: Creativity and Innovation (1a,1b), Technology Operations and Concepts (6a, 6b)

21st Century Skills: Communication, collaboration, creativity, and innovation

Activity Overview

In this activity, students will be given an opportunity to listen to audio directions to complete a science lab activity. The students will then create an electronic lab report that summarizes their experiment.

Procedure

1. Place students into cooperative learning groups with an iPod. Ask them to listen to the directions for the lab activity as they go through the steps to complete the lab.

2. Ask students to use their cell phones to take photographs of the different stages of the experiment. Ask students to upload the photographs to Photobucket and then download the photos to a school computer.

3. After students have completed the experiment, ask them to use an iPod with a voice recorder to summarize their findings (the conclusions) of the experiment.

4. Ask students to upload their pictures and the MP3 audio file to their computer and create a short iMovie that summarizes their experiment.

5. Upload student movies to a class website, YouTube, or SchoolTube channel for sharing with other students.

Extension

1. Do the same activity with any content area, and include video.

2. Ask students to create a science safety podcast or iMovie for sharing with other students.

iPod Touch Vocabulary Study Lesson Plan

Content Area: All contents (vocabulary study)

Grade Levels: 3–12

Features and Materials: iPod touch, Google Docs (Spreadsheet), Laptops, GFlashApp, and Wi-Fi Internet access

ISTE Standards: Creativity and Innovation (1a, 1b), Research and Information Fluency (3b), Technology Operations and Concepts (6a, 6b)

21st Century Skills: Communication and collaboration

Activity Overview

In this activity, students will summarize definitions of vocabulary words and create electronic flash cards to use when studying.

Before the Lesson

1. Set up a free Google account at www.google.com by selecting the Gmail link on the top left of the screen and then choosing "Sign up for Gmail."

2. After you set up Gmail, select the Documents link to set up your Google Docs, which allows you to create and edit spreadsheets.

3. Download the free GFlash app to all iPod touch devices you wish to use.

4. Go to Gwhizmobile.com/desktop/creating.php and download the flash card template form that works with Google Spreadsheet.

5. Create a spreadsheet in Google Docs, and name the spreadsheet for the unit of study, for example, "Geometry Ch. 2 Vocabulary."

Procedure

Help each student create his or her own Google account in class. In Google Docs, invite all students to contribute to the Google Spreadsheet.

1. Place students into several small groups of two or three. Assign each group to a laptop. Give each group equal amounts of vocabulary words that are related to the current unit of study.

2. Have each group open the Google spreadsheet. Explain to students that they will enter vocabulary words in column A and a summarized definition for each vocabulary word in column B of the Google Spreadsheet. All students will contribute to the same document at the same time. Ask students to take turns using the flash cards by asking each other questions.

Extension

1. There are several options on GFlash that students can use with the flash cards, for example, multiple-choice function and reverse question and answers.

2. Ask two students to select vocabulary words and compare their similarities and differences on a Venn diagram.

3. Students can add pictures and sound to the cards or even a third and fourth side to a card.

iPad Current Events Jigsaw Lesson Plan

Content Area: Social Studies

Grade Levels: 3–12

Features and Materials: ABC News app

ISTE Standards: Communication and Collaboration (2b), Research and Information Fluency (3b)

21st Century Skills: Communication and collaboration

Activity Overview

In this activity, students will complete a jigsaw reading activity using the ABC News app.

Procedure

1. Ask students to select two or three or related articles to read from the ABC News app.

2. After each student is placed in a heterogeneous reading group equal to the number of articles selected, ask students to read the article silently that they will share with the group.

3. Have each student take notes to assist with retelling the article and answering questions related to the article. After all students have completed reading the articles silently, have one of the members of the group begin retelling the article. The other members of the group take notes while the other member is retelling the article.

4. Ask students to draw conclusions from the series of articles that were read and select an article (other than their own) and use their notes to summarize.

5. Ask students to complete an exit card as an assessment. Students should indicate three new pieces of information they learned from the reading, two questions they have as a result of the reading, and one piece of information related to the reading that they knew prior to the activity.

Extension

After they've read the articles, ask students to participate in a Socratic seminar in which they answer real-world questions, closed-ended questions, open-ended questions, and general theme questions.

Nintendo DS Pictochat Math Lesson Plan

Content Area: Math

Grade Levels: All

Features and Materials: Nintendo DS and Pictochat

ISTE Standards: Communication and Collaboration (2b), Research and Information Fluency (3b)

21st Century Skills: Critical thinking, communication, and collaboration

Activity Overview

In this activity, students will work collaboratively in groups to solve math problems. Students will share answers electronically with the teacher.

Procedure

1. Create at least four workstations. Take a math worksheet that has several problems on it, and divide the worksheet into the same number of parts that you have created workstations for. Post the divided questions at each workstation. Divide students into four cooperative groups.

2. Give each group a Nintendo DS, and assign each group one of the four Pictochat rooms (A, B, C or D). Tell students that they have to whisper to each other while at each station and that they cannot communicate verbally with the teacher. All communication to the teacher has to be through Pictochat. Ask students to start at a station and begin to work out the problems. When the group has an answer to a problem, ask them to write the number of the problem and the answer to the problem in the Pictochat field, then enter "Send."

3. Open each Pictochat room periodically throughout the activity to check the groups' answers. Let the groups know if the answer is correct or not by writing "correct" or "try again" in the Pictochat field, then hit "Send" to send the response back to the group. You can also coach them by writing help hints and sending them to the group.

4. Rotate students after an appropriate amount of time.

5. Use the transcript of the answers to assess each group.

Extension

1. Give written feedback via the Pictochat as groups are working.

2. Use the Pictochat function with individual students in a small group of four.

Sony PSP Vocabulary Book Lesson Plan

Content Area: All

Grade Levels: 3–12

Features and Materials: Sony PSP and PowerPoint

ISTE Standards: Communication and Collaboration (2b), Research and Information Fluency (3b), Technology Operations and Concepts (6b)

21st Century Skills: Critical thinking and creativity and innovation

Activity Overview

In this activity, students will create an electronic ABC vocabulary book that focuses on key events, characters, ideas, and information from a unit of study.

Procedure

1. Ask students to create a list of words, using the entire alphabet, that relate to the unit of study for each letter (for example, in an astronomy unit, A—asteroid, B—black hole, C—constellation, and so on).

2. Ask students to create simple definitions that an elementary student could understand for each term and identify a picture that could be used to accompany the term.

3. Ask students to create a PowerPoint that includes twenty-seven slides. The first slide should include a title; the other twenty-six slides will be for the pages of the book (one for each letter of the alphabet).

4. Each page of the electronic book should include the vocabulary word, a picture, and an example.

5. Once the PowerPoint is completed, ask students to save the PowerPoint as JPEG images. The file can then be transferred to the Sony PSP and shared with other classmates.

Extension

1. Ask students to create study cards for units using the same methods.

2. Ask students to write short stories using unit vocabulary and share them with classmates.

eReader (iPad) iBook Literature Circles Lesson Plan

Content Area: All

Grade Levels 2–12

Features and Materials: An eReader, iBook app, and downloaded iBooks

ISTE Standards: Communication and Collaboration (2b), Research and Information Fluency (3b)

21st Century Skills: Critical thinking and communication

Activity Overview

In this activity, students will clarify word meaning and pronunciation by participating in a literature circle.

Procedure

1. Select a book for students to read, and load the book onto an iBook app (with iPad). Arrange students into small heterogeneous groups.

2. Give students a graphic organizer that includes the following columns:

    a. Word

    b. Definition

    c. Synonym

    d. Sentence from book

3. In the small group, read the section together. Pause periodically as students come to unfamiliar words.

4. Take turns selecting students to identify the definition of the unfamiliar word by holding their finger on the word and selecting "Dictionary." Ask students to add details to their graphic organizers for the unfamiliar words.

5. Take turns discussing the meaning of vocabulary words by using context clues.

6. Allow students time to discuss the selected reading.

Extension

Ask students to identify a word in the chapter and select the "Search" function to find the word in other sections of the book. Ask students to read the other identified sentences to gather meaning from context.

Netbook Glogster Movie Poster Lesson Plan

Content Area: Language Arts

Grade Levels: 3–8

Features and Materials: Netbook with Internet access, chapter book or novel, and Glogster account (edu.glogster.com)

ISTE Standards: Creativity and Innovation (1a, 1b), Research and Information Fluency (3b), Techology Operations and Concepts (6a, 6b)

21st Century Skills: Communication, collaboration, and creating

Activity Overview

In this activity students will summarize a book that they have read by creating a movie poster that advertises the book.

Procedure

1. Before class, open an educator Glogster account at edu.glogster.com. Add students to your account.

2. After students have read their book, have them identify their favorite scene from the book. Tell students that they should use their favorite scene as the main visual for the movie poster.

3. Have students use the text function to write a short summary of the book and quotes from some of the characters.

4. Have students import download photographs, sound files, and video from the internet to include with their poster.

Extension

1. Before class, open an educator Glogster account at edu.glogster.com. Add students to your account.

2. Have students dress up as characters in the book and act out a favorite scene. Students can videotape a short scene and upload it to their movie Glogster.

Implications of Mobile Learning

Learning is quite personal. We all have learning-style preferences that are enhanced when learning is rigorous, engaging, and relevant. m-Learning promotes those aspects of learning for students, and for that reason, it represents the next stage in learning with technology. Although: technology by itself does not guarantee learning, when effectively used, it can help focus attention and maintain interest. To reiterate, mobile learning used with instruction has the following tangible benefits:

- **Varied learning conditions**—Using mobile learning can allow students to be immersed in virtual environments and to provide instances where they can master skills at their own pace and in places where they are most comfortable.

- **Opportunities for collaboration**—Mobile learning methodologies are best used as part of other learning strategies and when combined with group activities, paper-based materials, and traditional educational activities. Educators can use MLDs to promote one of the most important 21st century skills: working collaboratively.

- **Day-to-day learning**—It is normal see cell towers disguised as pine trees in the north and palm trees in the south. This practice is an indication of how m-learning devices have permeated our society (Librero et al., 2007). Educators can leverage the ubiquity of MLDs, which allows 24/7 access to information.

- **Instant feedback**—Sharing work, such as writing, video, music, and art, permit almost instant feedback from those using the same platform. The continuous stimulus and response students experience in gaming appears to intensify their need—and expectation—for fast feedback and reinforcement. The feedback students receive in class is also expected to be purposeful, so students can improve on their performance.

- **Authenticity of learning**—Because learning with mobile learning devices occurs in real time, the experience is considered relevant and authentic by those who are learning. Mobile learning for today's generation reinforces authenticity by allowing students to multitask and network with others—it is real learning. One benefit of mobile learning that we often overlook is that the real-world experience of interacting with others with similar interests allows learning to happen as the learner needs it to happen. This is why students today don't immediately grab the user's manual. They explore the tool first, problem solve as situations arrive, and then share solutions with others.

Recognizing that there are several benefits to using mobile learning, the challenge is deciding how to embrace and manage this paradigm when teaching. This has to be done through purposeful professional development.

Professional Development for MLDs

If mobile learning devices are to be used purposefully, educators have to be made aware of the instructional benefits as well as the disadvantages. Teachers need to participate in ongoing professional development that teaches them to see these devices as mobile learning computers and not just as gadgets. Professional development will be essential in making or breaking the attitudes toward using these tools in the classroom.

As an instructional leader, identify those "rock star" teachers who can make other teachers comfortable with the concept of using mobile learning devices. These are the teachers who will be able to build capacity. The most challenging aspect of implementing mobile learning (or anything new for that matter) is getting started. Hands-on activities and experimentation are highly recommended. Have teachers experience the very tools they will be using. Ask them to bring their cell phones to an afterschool workshop to experience some of the same activities that they might later ask students to do. A simple activity using polleverywhere.com with staff can bring the wow factor to any faculty meeting. For example, at an end-of-year staff meeting, principals can use polleverywhere to engage staff in identifying the professional development focus for the following school year. The results could be used to generate a robust conversation about professional development. Adults need and appreciate having the time to be creative, to play, and to reflect on their experiences so that they can realize the potential of these tools in their classrooms.

In addition to teachers needing professional development for integrating technology, administrators have to model it. Alan November once told our district administrators at a summer retreat that if we wanted teachers to utilize technology, principals had to model its use, and to model its use, they had to have time to experience technology. So we set up what we referred to as the Principal's Digital Playground series. We invited principals to come and play with technology and experience web 2.0 tools to see how they could use them with their work. This kind of hands-on experience is valuable for all educators.

Potential for Education Reform

Ownership of mobile devices among children has shown a steady increase since 2005 (Shuler, 2009). These devices allow students to be connected to a world outside the four walls of their schools and homes. They can open up worlds for children who come from impoverished backgrounds, who are understimulated at home and unsupported in learning. It goes without saying that additional research and development are needed in order to determine how mobile learning devices can become a key factor in how we integrate technology into education to reform the way we teach. However, research that does exist indicates that content experts believe MLDs have significant potential to transform children's learning. Although content experts believe in the potential of mobile learning, that is not always true with noneducators. In order for mobile learning to be truly considered to be a key factor in helping to reform education, public perception about mobile learning has to change. We have to alter beliefs that cell phones in school are evil and that social networking is only for bad people.

The way that we change these beliefs is to first change practice. I attended a conference at which Tom Guskey was the keynote speaker. In his speech, he said that for change to happen, we have to get people to act their way into thinking rather than to try to get people to think their way into acting (Guskey, 2010). By having students use MLDs on a regular and consistent basis (acting), perceptions (thinking) are bound to change. If our thinking changes, then so will other factors that could have an effect on education reform using technology integration. The change in thinking is gradual, but it is happening. For example, the Virginia Department of Education sponsored a contest for applications developers to create an iPod touch application that focused on sixth-grade social studies content. Three winning entries received monetary awards ranging from $15,000 (and a contract to work with a larger developing company) to $5,000 for a third-place entry.

Businesses are changing their thinking and becoming involved as well. Why? It is estimated that education worldwide is a $2.5 trillion business. Why not? Cell-phone-service-providing companies are targeting younger consumers in order to increase the likelihood of what they refer to as brand loyalty. T-Mobile once launched a promotion that enabled students to get free phones. The advertisement mentioned that anyone signing up by a specific date would be eligible to get up to three free lines.

Some would argue that cell phone companies are looking at educational ventures for corporate profits. I don't disagree. I would argue, however, that the same was true of computer companies several years ago. Based on the history of the business of technology and the business of education, it is evident to me that the business of merging education and mobile learning devices to help reform education is a goldmine waiting to be discovered.

As we search for technological solutions for our education problems, which appear to continually increase, the data tell us that mobile learning not only appeals to kids of today, it helps with academic achievement. I recently came across several projects involving mobile learning that are beginning to surface. For example, Project K-Nect (Project Tomorrow, 2010) is a program being conducted in Onslow County, North Carolina. Teachers there have been using smartphones to teach students algebra. Initial results indicate that significant increases in student achievement came about as a result of their experiences. Empirical data regarding mobile learning is more prevalent in other countries. A recent Consolarium study (National Learning Assessment, 2010) in Scotland noted that children's ability to calculate accurately rocketed, as did their speed of processing, after using Nintendo DS programs regularly over the course of eight to ten weeks.

Two West Virginia Elementary schools received a $42,000 grant from Verizon Wireless to fund a mobile learning project using cell phones for their fifth-grade students. The project was designed to expand learning in the classroom for students who had limited access to the Internet. Similar projects are continuing to spring up around the country to support student learning.

Mobile-learning mania is imminent. The number of mobile-phone subscribers was expected to reach five billion during 2010 (British Broadcasting Corporation, 2010). The U.S. Department of Education has designated nearly $5 billion in competitive school-reform grants to scale up pilot programs and to evaluate best practices of all kinds (U.S. Department of Education, 2009). I am predicting mobile learning will be a major part of that initiative.

A Fundamental Shift

We have to recognize that technology itself is only a minimal part of the solution for ensuring a highly effective education and that a significant change in the way we do business needs to be made if we are to truly prepare students for the 21st century workforce. At issue is an extremely deep cultural shift, a fundamental rethinking not only of how education is delivered, but also of what education means today. Putting mobile learning into practice—really bringing about pedagogical change and placing students in the driver's seat of their own education—will be arduous.

Mobile learning challenges many of the basic assumptions that have been made for decades about education. It challenges what it means to learn and what it means to teach. Mobile learning challenges the accumulated research and traditional mortar and brick spaces where established pedagogies and the value of traditional tools and resources have been commonplace.

As a principal, it's unsettling to think of being responsible for organizing a framework that teachers will use to prepare students for the 21st century workforce. Even more distressing is that we still have difficulty identifying consistent definitions for 21st century teaching and learning and for the 21st century instructional practices we must have to get students where they need to be. The focus of instruction has to be on how to integrate new technology with proven high-yield instructional strategies.

The good news is that, although fear of the unknown is difficult to avoid, whenever you have an opportunity to observe a student eagerly embracing an iPod touch to reinforce multiplication facts or conducting research using a Netbook while outside on a warm spring day, it is difficult not to become excited about the possibilities of delivering good instruction with the assistance of mobile learning devices.

REFERENCES AND RESOURCES

Aderinoye, R. A., Ojokheta, K. O., & Olojede, A. A. (2007). Integrating mobile learning into nomadic education programme in Nigeria: Issues and perspectives. *International Review of Research in Open and Distance Learning, 8*(2), 1–17.

Alexander, B. (2004). Going nomadic: Mobile learning in higher education. *EDUCAUSE Review, 39*(5), 28–35.

Anderson, J. (2005, August 22). New study recasts cell phones as effective teaching tool. *Ergonomics Today.* Accessed at www.ergoweb.com/news/detail.cfm?id=1180 on February 11, 2011.

Andone, D., Dron, J., Pemberton, L., & Boyne, C. (2007). E-learning environments for digitally-minded students. *Journal of Interactive Learning Research, 18*(1), 41–53.

Baker, J. (2009, August 13). *New school cell phone policy.* Accessed at www.wowt.com/news/headlines /53165407.htm1 on July 15, 2010.

British Broadcasting Coportation. (2010). *Over 5 billion mobile phone connections worldwide.* BBC Mobile. Accessed at www.bbc.co.uk/news/10569081 on April 19, 2011.

Brown, T. H. (2003, June). *The role of m-learning in the future of e-learning in Africa?* Paper presented at the 21st ICDE World Conference, Hong Kong, China.

Çavus, N., Bicen, H., & Akçil, U. (2008, June). *The opinions of information technology students on using mobile learning.* Paper presented at the 2008 International Conferences on Educational Sciences, Magusa, North Cyprus.

Celizic, M. (2009). *Her teen committed suicide over sexting.* Accessed at http://today.msnbc.msn.com/id /29546030/ns/today-parenting on November 23, 2010.

Charmonman, S., & Chorpothong, N. (2005). *Digital lifestyle and the road ahead.* Proceedings of the Fourth International Conference on eBusiness, December 5–9. Beijing, China. Accessed at www .charm.ksc.au.edu/SCPaper/Digital%20Lifestyle%20and%20the%20Road%20Ahead.pdf on April 24, 2010.

Christen, A. (2009). Transforming the classroom for collaborative learning in the 21st century. *Techniques: Connecting Education and Careers, 84*(1), 28–31.

Cmuk, D., Mutapcic, T., & Borsic, M. (2007). *Mobile measurement support for remote laboratories and e-learning systems.* Proceedings of the16th IMEKO TC4 Symposium Exploring New Frontiers of Instrumentation and Methods for Electrical and Electronic Measurements September 22–24, 2008, Florence, Italy. Accessed at www.imeko.org/publications/tc4–2008/IMEKO-TC4–2008–204. pdf on April 24, 2010.

Common Sense Media. (2010). *Do smart phones = smart kids?* San Francisco: Author.

Corbeil, J., & Valdes-Corbeil, M. (2007). Are you ready for mobile learning? *EDUCAUSE Quarterly, 30*(2), 51–58.

CTIA: The Wireless Association & Harris Interactive. (2008). *A generation unplugged.* Washington, DC: Authors. Accessed at http://files.ctia.org/pdf/HI_TeenMobileStudy_ResearchReport.pdf on February 14, 2011.

Deubel, P. (2009, March 19). Mobile devices: Facing challenges and opportunities for learning. *The Journal.* Accessed at www.thejournal.com/articles/24153 on February 11, 2011.

Dodds, R., & Mason, C. Y. (2005). Cell phones and PDA's hit k–6. *Education Digest, 70*(8), 52–53.

Duke Center for Instructional Technology. (2008). *Mobile devices in education.* Accessed at http://cit.duke.edu/tools/mobile/index.html on August 10, 2010.

Elliott, W. (2006). The audiocast diaries: Reflections on radio and podcasting for delivery of educational soap operas. *International Review of Research in Open and Distance Learning, 7*(3), 1–11.

Fallon, J. (2008). Lost in web 2.0 cyberspace? *Principal Leadership, 9*(4), 68–70.

Gilroy, M. (2004). Invasion of the classroom cell phones. *Education Digest, 69*(6), 59–60.

Goh, T., & Hooper, V. (2007). To txt or not to txt: That's the puzzle. *Journal of Information Technology Education, 6,* 441–453.

Grimes, C. (2009, April 6). Cell phones get top marks in class. *Daily Press.* Accessed at http://edtechblog.jacquelinemorris.com/2009/04/cell-phones-get-top-marks-in-class.html on June 3, 2011.

Guskey, T. (2010, October 8). *Keynote address: Assessment and Evaluation for Learning National Evaluation institute.* Consortium for Research on Educational Accountability & Teacher Evaluation Conference; College of William and Mary, Williamsburg, VA.

Guy, R. (Ed.). (2009). *The evolution of mobile teaching and learning.* Santa Rosa, CA: Informing Science Press.

Harley, D., Winn, S., Pemberton, S., & Wilcox, P. (2007). Using texting to support students' transition to university. *Innovations in Education and Teaching International, 44*(3), 229–241.

Hupp, S. (2009, March 5). Texting in class sparks bill to ban cell phones. *Des Moines Register.* Accessed at www.districtadministration.com/newssummary.aspx?news=yes&postid=52053 on July 2, 2010.

Institute for Global Education and Service-Learning (n.d.) *Service learning is good brain-based learning.* Accessed at www.youthactioncouncil.org/Resources/Clemsonsisl/BrainBasedLearning.pdf on August 1, 2010.

International Society for Technology in Education. (2010). *Standards for global learning in the digital age.* Accessed at www.iste.org/AM/Template.cfm?Section=NETS on February 14, 2011.

Jensen, E. (2008). *Brain-based learning: The new paradigm of teaching* (2nd ed.). Thousand Oaks, CA: Corwin Press.

Jensen, E. (2010, February 5). *Factors that contribute most to student achievement.* Accessed at www.jensenlearning.com/news/factors-that-contribute-most-to-student-achievement/brain-based-teaching on July 12, 2010.

Johnson, C., & Kritsonis, W. A. (2007). National school debate: Banning cell phones on public school campuses in America. *National Forum of Educational Administration and Supervision Journals, 25*(4), 1–6.

Kaser, D. (2009). Focusing on ejournals (and blogging at the same time). *Computers in Libraries, 29*(2), 33–35.

Kay, K. (2010). 21st century skills: Why they matter, what they are, and how we got there. In J. Bellanca & R. Brandt (Eds.), *21st century skills: Rethinking how students learn* (pp. xiii–xxxi). Bloomington, IN: Solution Tree Press.

Kolb, L. (2006). From toy to tool: Audioblogging with cell phones. *Learning and Leading With Technology, 34*(3), 16–20.

Kolb, L. (2008). *Toys to tools: Connecting student cell phones to education.* Eugene, OR: International Society for Technology in Education.

Lenhart, A. (2010). *Cell phones and American adults.* Washington, DC: Pew Research Center. Accessed at www.pewInternet.org/Reports/2010/Cell-Phones-and-American-Adults.aspx on February 14, 2011.

Lenhart, A., Ling, R., Campbell, S., & Purcell, K. (2010). *Teens and mobile phones.* Washington, DC: Pew Research Center. Accessed at www.pewinternet.org/~/media//Files/Reports/2010/PIP-Teens-and -Mobile-2010-with-topline.pdf on September 17, 2010.

Librero, F., Ramos, A., Ranga, A., Triñona, J., & Lambert, D. (2007). Uses of the cell phone for education in the Philippines and Mongolia. *Distance Education, 28*(2), 231–244.

Mario, D. (2008, February 15). Students phoning it in. *Leader-Post.* Accessed at www2.canada.com/ reginaleaderpost/news/story.html?id=cf9045aa-bbf7–40f6–820b-0fab7e7e2d22&k=68380 onAugust 10, 2010.

Marzano, R. (2003). *What works in schools: Translating research into action.* Alexandria, VA: Association for Supervision and Curriculum Development.

Marzano, R., Pickering, D. J., & Pollock, J. E. (2001). *Classroom instruction that works: Research-based strategies for increasing student achievement.* Alexandria, VA: Association for Supervision and Curriculum Development.

McGuire, L. (2005). Assessment using new technology. *Innovations in Education and Teaching International, 42*(3), 265–276.

McNeal, T., & van 't Hooft, M. (2006). Anywhere, anytime: Using mobile phones for learning. *Journal of the Research Center for Educational Technology, 2*(2), 24–31. Accessed at www.rcetj.org/index.php /rcetj/article/view/91/139 on January 18, 2011.

McTighe, J., & Seif, E. (2010). An implementation framework to support 21st century skills. In J. Bellanca & R. Brandt (Eds.), *21st century skills: Rethinking how students learn* (pp. 149–172). Bloomington, IN: Solution Tree Press.

Millard Public Schools. (2010). *Millard North High School 2010–2011 student & parent guide.* Accessed at http://mps.mnhs.schoolfusion.us/modules/groups/homepagefiles/cms/750501/File /Publications/10–11%20Student%20Handbook%20Revised%20by%20Phipps%206–24–10%20 w%20grey.pdf?sessionid=d53d73513bc7c912947d5c681d051224 on September 17, 2010.

Mishra, P., & Koehler, M. J. (2006). Technological Pedagogical Content Knowledge: A new framework for teacher knowledge. *Teachers College Record, 108*(6), 1017–1054.

Moore, A., & Ahonen, T. (2004). *SMLXtralarge.* Accessed at http://smlxtralarge.com/2004/03/11/mobile-marketing-how-to-succeed-in-a-connected-age on December 12, 2009.

Mostakhdemin-Hosseini, A., & Tuimala, J. (2005, June). *Mobile learning framework.* Presented at the IADIS International Conference on Mobile Learning, Qawra, Malta.

Motiwalla, L. F. (2007). Mobile learning: A framework and evaluation. *Computers & Education, 49*(3), 581–596.

Naismith, L., Lonsdale, P., Vavoula, G., & Sharples, M. (2004). *Futurelab Series Report 11: Literature review in mobile technologies and learning.* Bristol, England: Futurelab. Accessed at www2.futurelab.org.uk/resources/documents/lit_reviews/Mobile_Review.pdf on January 18, 2011.

National Learning Assessment. (2010). *Games-based learning research by Scottish academics to be published in renowned education journal.* Accessed at www.ltscotland.org.uk/newsandevents/educationnews/2010/pressreleases/july/news_tcm4621428.asp on September 17, 2010.

Neil, M. (2008). *Friends' mom charged with fraud over MySpace cyberbullying suicide.* Accessed at www.abajournal.com/news/article/friends_mom_charged_with_fraud_over_myspace_cyberbullying_suicide on November 14, 2010.

New Media Consortium & EDUCAUSE Learning Initiative. (2007). *The Horizon Report: 2007 edition.* Austin, TX: New Media Consortium. Accessed at www.nmc.org/pdf/2007_Horizon_Report.pdf on February 14, 2011.

Nielsen Mobile. (2007). *Mobile audio is a significant growth opportunity says Arbitron/Telephia study* [Press release]. Accessed at www.telephia.com/html/FirstfindingsArbitron_Telephia_Mobile_Audio_Release_FINAL_3–26–07.html on February 14, 2011.

Partnership for 21st Century Skills. (2008). Framework for 21st century learning. Accessed at www.p21.0rg/documents/21st_century_skills_education_and_competitiveness_guide.pdf on May 6, 2010.

Peters, K. (2007). M-learning: Positioning educators for a mobile, connected future. *International Review of Research in Open and Distance Learning, 8*(2), 1–17.

Piecka, D., Studnicki, E., & Zuckerman-Parker, M. (2008). A proposal for ozone science podcasting in a middle science classroom. *Association for the Advancement of Computing in Education Journal, 16*(2), 203–233.

Plester, B., & Wood, C. (2009). Exploring relationships between traditional and new media literacies: British preteen texters at school. *Journal of Computer-Mediated Communication, 14*(4), 1108–1129.

Plunkett, L. (2009, May 11). One in five Japanese people now own a Nintendo DS. *Kotaku.* Accessed at www.kotaku.com.au/2009/05/one-in-five-japanese-people-now-own-a-nintendo-ds/ on February 14, 2011.

Prensky, M. (2005). What can you learn from a cell phone? Almost anything! *Innovate, 1*(5). Accessed at http://innovateonline.info/pdf/v0ll_issue5/What_Can_You_Learn_from_a_Cell_Phone__Almost_Anything!.pdf on January 18, 2011.

Project Tomorrow. (2010). *Project K-Nect evaluation report.* Accessed at www.tomorrow.org/docs /Project_K-Nect_EvaluationReport_Final_Ju17.pdf on April 8, 2011.

Rahulioizm. (2008, July 28). *Million* [Video file]. Accessed at www.youtube.com/watch?v=21z-9X_- 31U&feature=player_embedded on February 14, 2011.

Richtel, M. (2004, September 29). Schools relax cellphone bans, nodding to trend. *New York Times.* Accessed at www.nytimes.com/2004/09/29/national/29cellphone.html on February 14, 2011.

Richtel, M., & Stone, B. (2009, February 15). Industry makes pitch that smartphones belong in classroom. *New York Times.* Accessed at www.nytimes.com/2009/02/16/technology/16phone.html on February 14, 2011.

Rideout, V. J., Foehr, U. G., & Roberts, D. F. (2010). *Generation M²: Media in the lives of 8- to 18-year-olds: A Kaiser Family Foundation study.* Menlo Park, CA: Author. Accessed at www.kff.org/entmedia /upload/8010.pdf on February 14, 2011.

Rismark, M., Sølverg, A. M., Strømme, A., & Hokstad, L. M. (2007). Using mobile phones to prepare for university lectures: Student's experiences. *Turkish Online Journal of Educational Technology, 6*(4). Accessed at www.tojet.net/articles/649.pdf on January 18, 2011.

Roberts, D. F., & Foehr, U. G. (2008). Trends in media use. *Future of Children, 18*(1), 11–37.

Rogers, K. (2009a). Cell phones as instructional tools. *Principal Leadership, 9*(6), 65–67.

Rogers, K. (2009b). *Mobile learning using cell phones: Activities for the classroom.* Eugene, OR: Visions.

Rosenberger, B. (2010, August 18). Fifth graders to receive smartphones from Verizon. *The Herald-Dispatch.* Accessed at www.herald-dispatch.com/news/briefs/x254023064/Fifth-graders-to -receive-Smartphones-from-Verizon?i=0 on January 12, 2011.

Sadik, A. (2008). Digital storytelling: A meaningful technology-integrated approach for engaged student learning. *Educational Technology Research and Development, 56*(4), 487–506.

Schroeder, R. (2005). Prep pioneer taps tech trend to reach busy students. *Online Learning Update.* Accessed at http://people.uis.edu/rschr1/onlinelearning/archive/2006_02_26_archive.html on January 26, 2009).

Setzer, J. (2008, March 18). *$100 laptop vs. the mobile phone.* Accessed at http://huddlemind. com/2008/03/18/100-laptop-vs-the-mobile-phone on May 6, 2010.

Shuler, C. (2009). *Pockets of potential: Using mobile technologies to promote children's learning.* New York: Joan Ganz Cooney Center.

Skinner, B. F. (1965). *Science and human behavior.* Glencoe, IL: Free Press.

Sousa, D. (2001). *How the brain learns.* Thousand Oaks, CA: Corwin Press.

Soloway, E. (Writer), Norris, C. (Writer), & Cooper, D. (Director). (2009). Educating the mobile generation [Documentary film series episode]. In S. Brown (Executive producer), *A 21st century education.* Mill Valley, CA: Mobile Learning Institute. Accessed at http://newlearninginstitute.org /21stcenturyeducation/21st-century-learning/educating-the-mobile-generation.html on February 14, 2011.

Spender, D. (2007). *Digital literacies.* Accessed at www.dalespender.com/?new_wealth:digital_literacies on February 11, 2011.

Spriggs, M. (2010, March 23). McDonald's Japan to train staff using DS. *Weekly Word News.* Accessed at http://weeklyworldnews.com/headlines/16591/mcdonalds-japan-to-train-staff-using-ds on February 14, 2011.

Stansbury, M. (2008, March 11). Cell phones in schools: Opportunity or distraction? *eSchool News.* Accessed at www.eschoolnews.com/conference-info/cosn/cosn-news/index.cfm?i=53013 on February 14, 2011.

Stockwell, G. (2007). Vocabulary on the move: Investigating an intelligent mobile phone-based vocabulary tutor. *Computer Assisted Language Learning, 20*(4), 365–383.

Strom, P. S., & Strom, R. D. (2005). When teens turn cyberbullies. *Education Digest, 71*(4), 35–41.

Taaffe, O. (2006). Reach for your handset. *Telecommunications* [International Edition], *40*(4) 20–21.

Teaching Today. (n.d.). *Cell phones in the classroom.* Accessed at http://teachingtoday.glencoe.com/howtoarticles/cell-phones-in-the-classroom on February 14, 2011.

Thornton, P., & Houser, C. (2005). Using mobile phones in English education in Japan. *Journal of Computer Assisted Learning, 21*(3), 217–228.

TPACK. (2010). *Technological Pedagogical Content Knowledge.* Accessed at http://tpack.org/tpck/index.php?title=TPCK:About on February 14, 2011.

U.S. Department of Education (2009). *President Obama, U.S. Secretary of Education Duncan announce national competition to advance school reform.* Accessed at www.ed.gov/news/press-releases/president-obama-us-secretary-education-duncan-announce-national-competition-adva on April 20, 2011.

Vavoula, G., Sharples, M., Lonsdale, P., Rudman, P., & Meek, J. (2007). Learning bridges: A role for mobile technologies in education. *Educational Technology, 47*(3), 33–37.

Wagner, E. D. (2005). Enabling mobile learning. *EDUCAUSE Review, 40*(3), 40–53.

Wagner, E. D., & Robson, R. (2005, January). *Education unplugged: Mobile learning comes of age.* Presented at the annual meeting of the National Learning Infrastructure Initiative, New Orleans, LA.

Walser, N. (2008). Teaching 21st century skills: What does it look like in practice? *Harvard Education Letter, 24*(5). Accessed at www.hepg.org/hel/article/184 on January 18, 2011.

Wang, Y., Wu, M., & Wang, H. (2009). Investigating the determinants and age and gender difference in the acceptance of mobile learning. *British Journal of Educational Technology, 40*(1), 92–118.

Zurita, G., Nussbaum, M., & Sharples, M. (2003). Encouraging face-to-face collaborative learning through the use of handheld computers in the classroom. In L. Chittaro (Ed.), *Proceedings of Mobile HCI 2003* (pp. 193–208). Berlin, Germany: Springer-Verlag.

INDEX

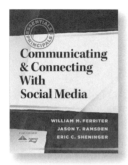

Communicating & Connecting With Social Media
William M. Ferriter, Jason T. Ramsden, and Eric C. Sheninger
Social media holds great potential benefits for schools reaching out to our communities, preparing our teachers, and connecting with our kids. In this short text, the authors examine how enterprising schools are using social media tools to provide customized professional development for teachers and to transform communication practices with staff, students, parents, and other stakeholders. **BKF475**

Teaching the iGeneration: Five Easy Ways to Introduce Essential Skills With Web 2.0 Tools
William M. Ferriter and Adam Garry
Find the natural overlap between the work you already believe in and the digital tools that define tomorrow's learning. Each chapter introduces an enduring life skill and a digital solution to enhance traditional skill-based instructional practices. A collection of handouts and supporting materials ends each chapter. **BKF393**

Creating a Digital-Rich Classroom: Teaching & Learning in a Web 2.0 World
Meg Ormiston
Instead of asking students to power down during class, power up your lesson plans with digital tools. Design and deliver lessons in which technology plays an integral role. Engage students in solving real-world problems while staying true to standards-aligned curricula. This book provides a research base and practical strategies for using web 2.0 tools to create engaging lessons that transform and enrich content. **BKF385**

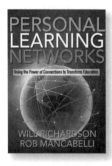

Personal Learning Networks: Using the Power of Connections to Transform Education
Will Richardson and Rob Mancabelli
The Internet connects us in unprecedented ways. To prepare students to flourish in this new learning world, schools will need to transform themselves in important ways. This book is a road map for any educator thinking about using the web for learning. Build your own learning network, and use learning networks in the classroom and schoolwide to improve student outcomes. **BKF484**

Innovation Through Technology: The Differentiators
Featuring Cheryl Lemke
Cheryl shows how to design tomorrow's curricula by using research in sociology, learning, and neuroscience to reinforce critical thinking, multitasking, multimodal learning, collaboration, and engagement. Connect the theory of 21st century skills to student learning and lesson design, and envision new designs for learning, made possible through digital tools. **DVF054**

Solution Tree | Press
a division of

Solution Tree

Visit solution-tree.com or call 800.733.6786 to order.

Solution Tree

Solution Tree's mission is to advance the work of our authors. By working with the best researchers and educators worldwide, we strive to be the premier provider of innovative publishing, in-demand events, and inspired professional development designed to transform education to ensure that all students learn.

The mission of the National Association of Elementary School Principals is to lead in the advocacy and support for elementary and middle level principals and other education leaders in their commitment for all children.